FREE BONUS— TRANSFORM YOUR LIFE

Sabine's topic, which she shares on stages around the world, is **communication and unlocking one's full potential**. She teaches us how to become better communicators, not only with others but also with ourselves.

As an actress, she learned how to slip into a role to think, feel, and act like that character. When we apply the same principles to our lives, we can literally **create what we want** in advance and thus experience its realization in the future.

Learning these actionable speaking, acting, and communication techniques will help you **become a competent and confident speaker and communicator** in your personal and business life.

Picture a day when you have the confidence to speak about your business everywhere you go, have all the clients you dreamed of, and have the financial freedom to live the life you imagine.

Visit the link below to access valuable resources, such as video tutorials, e-books, and interactive exercises on communication skills and self-talk.

Access the **FREE** content now:
sabinekvenberg.com/bookbonus

Book Sabine for Your Next Event

With Sabine Kvenberg's expertise and dynamic presentation style, audiences can expect transformative insights and actionable strategies to propel them toward success in both business and personal growth.

Here are some of Sabine's Keynote Topics:

- From Fear to Fame: Mastering Public Speaking with Confidence
- Authentic Connection in the Digital Age: Leveraging Video Content for Business Success
- Empowerment Through Communication: Unleashing Personal Growth and Confidence
- Communicate to Thrive: Essential Skills for Entrepreneurs and Small Business Owners

To book Sabine Kvenberg, contact her at
sabine@sabinekvenberg.com

PRAISE FOR
BECOME EMPOWERED

I am thrilled to endorse Sabine's powerful new book, *Become Empowered: Echoes Of Grace And Strength*. This inspiring collection of real-life stories is a testament to the resilience and strength of women, offering valuable insights and encouragement for anyone seeking their own transformation and triumph.

I know Sabine from her role as Music Minister for the church Unity of Fredericksburg, in Virginia, when I was a minister. Her musical gifts are many, but what makes her presentation extraordinary is how personal and authentic her music and message is. She thrives on coming to the edge of vulnerability and truth, so the audience is transfixed with the magic of authenticity.

This book takes that same spirit and inspires us with testimonies to the human spirit. One cannot read these stories without connecting in some way with each.

In a world that seems to emphasize the difficulties and challenges of life, one finds, in this book, that the soul is nurtured and inspired by women who have faced their inner demons and transcended them, opening new avenues of life and creative expression.
This is a book for our time and still resonates with the eternal wisdom of the strength of the human mind and soul that is forever overcoming its own self-imposed limitations.

—Rev. Juan Enrique Toro

I've had the thrill of meeting Sabine in person; she is a very vibrant being. I've seen her sing, dance, speak, and podcast, and now I've experienced Sabine's writing — Wow! What an uplifting book. Sabine's own story of becoming empowered has been an ongoing inspiration to me, and she writes about it beautifully in the first chapter. She connects with the reader through every word, sharing timeless, universal truths that will enrich my personal journey. Her encouraging words say it all: "When we embrace and enjoy the journey of becoming our next greater self, we cannot be anything but happy and grateful for this earthly experience." The following chapters are equally uplifting. Each author was carefully curated by Sabine, and you can tell because each story left me feeling inspired and ready to take on the world.

—**Jennifer Henczel, Podcaster,**
Author, and Founder of the
Women in Podcasting Network

What makes *Become Empowered* a standout piece is its ability to provide a beacon of light in times of darkness. These pages showcase that we're not alone in our struggles and how our resilience and grace can lead to profound transformation.

—**Renée Marino, International Speaker,**
Connection Expert & Best-Selling Author
of *Becoming a Master Communicator*

This book encourages us all to become greater than we imagined. The women are resilient, vulnerable, and changed forever. Their stories will inspire you to become who you were meant to be.

—**Jenny Alday Townend, Founder and CEO of Music Compound, Author and Podcaster**

The words in this book inspire and empower readers, igniting within them the same sense of limitless potential that Sabine ignited within me all those years ago.

—**Tiffany Lutz, MA**

I loved the idea of this book even before it was written. I've been looking forward to the finished product, and WOW, it completely exceeds my expectations! *Become Empowered* is a perfectly curated compilation of stories, all different yet echoing the same message. These ladies have some unique experiences to share, and they articulate them so beautifully that I feel empowered to face my deepest fears and roadblocks head-on and become all I can be!

Sabine and I have been friends and shared many stages in song. In fact, I was standing right next to her, encouraging and holding space for her during her story of vulnerability that she shares with us in this book. I can relate because I was feeling the same way! Self-doubt is a paralyzing emotion. Courage is the antidote. The women in this book are vulnerable, courageous, and victorious. You will be a different person after reading this book. Your fears and roadblocks will lose their hold on you, and your courage will be activated. Some books can change lives. This is one of them.

—**Dana Agnellini, Singer/Songwriter, Author**

BECOME
EMPOWERED

BECOME EMPOWERED
ECHOES OF GRACE AND STRENGTH

Real-Life Stories of Women's Transformation and Triumph

SABINE KVENBERG
with 12 Contributing Authors

Impact Publishers
Palmetto, Florida

Impact Publishers
Palmetto, Florida

Become Empowered: Echoes of Grace and Strength
Copyright © 2024 by Sabine Kvenberg
www.sabinekvenberg.com

Quantity discounts of this book are available. Personalized autographed copies are also available. Email publisher for more information.

Edited by: Sabine Kvenberg
Book designed by: Journey Bound Publishing

Print ISBN: 979-8-9903365-0-6
Ebook ISBN: 979-8-9903365-1-3
LCCN: 2024906561

First Edition
Printed in the United States of America

This book is dedicated to all the powerful women in the world who didn't take no for an answer, pushed through challenging times, and are the unknown heroes who lift others up.

CONTENTS

FOREWORD

SINCE THE FIRST time I met Sabine, it was evident that she was on a mission. Initially, the nature of this mission was unclear, but one thing was sure: Sabine was determined to find it, one way or another. When she launched her podcast "Become," it became apparent to me and everyone around her that she had found her mission and possessed a voice the world was ready to hear.

Personally, Sabine has been an inspiration to me. She consistently puts herself out there, ready to embrace new experiences and leap into the unknown. I am excited about her work because I know her voice will ignite inspiration in many others who are seeking to "Become".

I have been very fortunate to have had a front-row seat to witness Sabine's journey of self-empowerment and her impact on so many others through her work. This book is an extension of the energy that has permeated the halls of Podfest. I have become inspired by her incredible spirit and am truly grateful that she is sharing her gifts with the world.

Chris Krimitsos
Chief Creative Officer
www.PodfestExpo.com

PREFACE

IN MAY OF 2022, I attended the Podfest Expo in Orlando, Florida. There, Chris Krimitsos, the founder and CEO of this renowned event, inspired me to launch my own podcast. A month later, the inaugural episode of "BECOME" aired. The podcast features interviews with successful individuals from various industries, delving into their personal and professional journeys and the strategies they've used to achieve their goals. The podcast aims to inspire listeners to take steps towards reaching their own aspirations and becoming the best version of themselves.

Communication has always been a fundamental aspect of my life. As a professional actress and musical theater performer, I express myself through stories, songs, and roles in dramas and comedies. My experience as a business owner further honed my ability to connect with customers. Now, I share my insights on various global stages, helping thousands. I firmly believe that more effective communication can profoundly impact our world.

The growing number of downloads for my podcast made me realize the importance of these stories. They show listeners that they are not alone in their struggles. The heartfelt messages I received confirmed that these narratives made people feel heard and understood. This realization spurred me to gather more stories and invite some incredible women I've met to share their experiences in this book.

These stories resonate with many. They illuminate various contemporary issues and demonstrate that no matter how bleak a situation might seem, there is always a path to overcoming it. We are more resilient than we often believe. Each challenge helps us to grow. With growth comes progress, and with progress comes growth.

We must become the person we are meant to be to live the life we are destined to live.

These stories will not only entertain but also inspire. We are not alone in this journey called life. We have both seen and unseen guardian angels guiding us through our darkest times, helping us find the inner light that has always been within us. When we recognize and unleash our greatness, we become beacons for others, positively impacting the world.

Thank-Yous:

Firstly, I want to express my deepest gratitude to my husband, Mykal, for his unwavering support. He has always believed in me, never doubting my ability to achieve my dreams. His support has allowed me to maintain my free spirit, and he has been my rock in moments of self-doubt, always there to lift me up. He truly is the wind beneath my wings.

My life would not be the same without my family and friends, who have been my pillars of strength and encouragement. A big, heartfelt hug to my stepdad, whom I lovingly call Hubsi, who raised me from the age of five and replaced my birth father, whom I lost at the tender age of three. Hubsi drove me to sports events, played with me outside, and taught me how to skin dive during our summer vacations. He was there for me throughout my childhood and teenage years, from sports events to deep conversations. My heart still yearns for my mother, who left this earth 30 years ago. She always supported me and traveled the world to see me in plays I was in or directed. Mama, you will always stay close to my heart.

I am profoundly thankful to Reverend Trisha Mack Hamilton (rest in peace) for her significant role in my spiritual journey. My gratitude extends to Dana Agnellini, with whom I shared music and life's milestones. Dana encouraged me to record my first CD, leaving a lasting musical legacy. To my dear friends Sabrina, Lynnette, and Victoria: thank you for being those irreplaceable friends who are always there when needed.

Lastly, I am grateful to everyone who has touched my life, even briefly, helping me to find love in myself and see it in others.

Namaste,
Sabine Kvenberg

CURTAIN CALL FOR DESTINY: MY LIFE BEYOND THE OFFICE WINDOW

by Sabine Kvenberg

> When we give ourselves Grace, accept our fears and shortcomings, and see it as an opportunity to learn and grow, we can improve and try again.

AS I STARTED my life as a young adult, I followed my dad's well-meant advice: "Sabine, find a job with benefits and a good salary — so you can pay your bills and have something left over to pursue your hobbies." So, that is what I did. I took a position with a successful insurance company, working as a claim adjuster. I had a nice office on the 6th floor, with a window and view over Hamburg, Germany, but I was unhappy. This job was draining me. On one boring, miserable workday, I stared out the window, thinking I couldn't do this for the next 40 years. I asked myself, is this all there is for me? What options do I have? Ask, and ye shall receive. That same week, on my way home from work, I bumped into my former drama and music teacher, Mr. Herbst. We had a casual conversation, but when he asked me if I was still active with my performance group, I was overcome with a sad feeling. My answer was no. His reply stirred up my soul. He said, "What a shame, Sabine, you are so talented!" That one sentence changed my life. It was like waking up to the person I ought to be, using the gifts and talent I received from my creator. I love to sing, dance, and act. Although I had no clue how to get started in the entertainment industry, I took action. I auditioned for an acting school, got accepted, and 3 years later became a working actress.

Following my heart and pursuing my passion has always been the cornerstone of my life. I had a 10-year dream career as an actress and musical theater performer in Europe. During an international tour of *Fiddler On The Roof,* I met my now husband. In 1994, we moved to the US to start a performing arts school in Fredericksburg, Virginia, to pass on our love for the performing arts. I loved being a teacher. I quickly realized that I instructed more than acting, dance, and singing skills; I taught my students life lessons. Training aspiring performers to enter the entertainment industry was fulfilling. It was another way to use my talent and the gift my creator gave me.

In 2000 — the turn of the millennium — my life also took a turn. It was one of those beautiful fall days in Virginia. The leaves on the trees turned orange and red. I was sitting at the front desk of our performing arts school when a couple entered the front door. They introduced themselves as Tricia and Daniel Hamilton from Unity Church of Fredericksburg. After a friendly exchange of pleasantry, they asked: "We are looking to rent space for our Sunday services and are wondering if you are open to it?" I was more than open to it; I was looking for extra income, and renting out space would be perfect. We had a long conversation, and I am confident this would be a good partnership. We agreed. Little did I know that this agreement would lead to something even more significant.

Reverend Trica invited my husband and I to attend their first Sunday worship. We agreed. After all, we wanted to ensure that all was legit and that no funny business was happening. A couple of weeks later, they had their first service. Our dance studio was transformed into a sanctuary that day. A wooden lectern with flowers represented the fall season. Blue folding chairs were set in rows with the perfect distance between each other, purple material to cover the ballet barres brought in colors, and a beautiful tapestry of a painting by the artist Thomas Kinkade was hanging on the wall. We enjoyed the service and message. I was excited to learn more about this new Church in town.

We returned the following Sunday, and I felt I found a new spiritual home. That day, Reverend Tricia announced that the Church seeks a person to do the music ministry. Enthusiastically, I raised my hand, and a few weeks later, I became the music minister of Unity of Fredericksburg. I started taking classes and worked closely with Reverend Tricia. I ensured the music I picked and performed matched and enhanced her Sunday messages. I even began to compose music for our Sunday services. It was well received by our congregation.

After my third year as a music minister, I attended a conference for speakers and musicians at the headquarters of Unity Village in Kansas City, Missouri. On the second to the last day, we had "Spirit Sharing". All musicians' names were put in a hat for the chance to perform their original music on stage. There were about 100 musicians in the auditorium. I have never shared my music outside of our small congregation in Fredericksburg. As a trained singer and musical theater performer, I had no problem performing in front of an audience. After all, I performed in front of thousands of people. However, this time was different. I was about to share one of my songs that reflected my experiences. Thoughts went through my head like what if they don't like it, what if I mess up, and what if they laugh at me? Secretively, I wished my name would not be selected, and my wish came true. I was relieved but, at the same time, disappointed in myself for letting fear take over.

The next evening, we had two guest performers close the event. Gregg Temblin finished the performance with a song we all knew very well, *Heart of the Mother*. The entire audience joined, singing along. We all held hands. It was a magical moment. I felt so empowered until the MC said we would finish with all who could not perform the previous evening.

My heart started racing. The voices in my head were repeating the same sentences from the night before. What if... This time, I stopped myself. I responded differently. The energy I felt after singing along and the cheerful spiritedness in the room gave me the courage to respond to myself: "Sabine, if you don't get up now to perform in front of this supportive audience of fellow musicians, you will never do it. You will never give other people the opportunity to listen to your music. Remember, it's not about you but the message you ought to share.

My thoughts started returning to my dad. He always encouraged me to be brave and do my best. The last time I visited him, he told me that he wanted to downgrade and was about to move out of the home I grew up in. While there, he reminded me that my first guitar, which I had played as a teenager, was stacked away in the attic. "Why don't you take it with you? Playing an instrument is like riding a bike. You may get a little rusty, but it'll all come back to you." With my dad's words of encouragement echoing in my mind, I decided to bring the guitar back home and started playing again. I composed my first song on the guitar, "Hello Again." This was the song I chose to perform that evening.

A voice blasting from the sound system brought me back from my reminiscence. "Next up, Sabine Kvenberg." This was me. This was the moment. There was no turning back. I prayed to feel confident, to be myself, and for God to guide me. I took a deep breath, got up, grabbed my guitar, and walked onto the stage. People later lovingly shared that I looked like Maria from the Sound of Music with my skirt, blouse, and guitar. Standing before the microphone, I decided to speak from the heart. I told how I brought back my guitar from Germany and how I started playing and composing this song. I invited the audience to join me in singing during the chorus.

What happened then was nothing short of a miracle. When it came to the chorus, everyone sang along. Being in an auditorium packed with musicians, the harmonies were heavenly. I got a standing ovation. It was a great confirmation for me to keep going. At the end of the evening, many people approached me with positive comments: Thank you for sharing your message, thank you for this song, please keep writing, your music is needed, and so on. That was a confirmation for me to continue writing and sharing my positive and uplifting messages. I felt happy and at peace.

This is the song I shared that evening:

Hello Again (I Am) — © Sabine Kvenberg

This feeling inside can no longer hide
It wants to come out and play in my field of dreams
So free and so pure, my soul now can soar
Now I can see who I am

Chorus: I Am, I Am, I Am, I Am (2 x)

I'm learning each day to find the right way
Sometimes, I take detours, but my goal is clear

My senses grow strong, to where I belong
The circle of oneness is growing my way

Chorus: I Am, I Am, I Am, I Am (2 x)
Bridge: Joy overwhelms me when I align with Divine
      Distant memories whisper" Hello again" to my

Refrain: I Am, I Am, I Am, I Am (2 x) ©

I learned that evening that no matter how scared and nervous I was, I mustered the courage to step out of my comfort zone. At the same time, I allowed myself to fail as well. Most importantly, I felt that with my faith, "Spirit" would guide me in my pursuit, and I would overcome anything.

When we give ourselves Grace, accept our fears and short-comings, and see it as an opportunity to learn and grow, we can improve and try again. If we don't act because we are too scared, we never know if this will be what we need to do to move to the next level. Stepping into my fear was a catalyst to share my music more often, write more songs, and even produce my first CD. Interestingly enough, the title song of my CD was born the next day while I was still on Unity Village's sacred grounds. I had a few hours to spare before catching a cab to the airport. In front of the Church was a labyrinth walk. A labyrinth is used as a walking meditation. It is a single winding path from the outer edge to the center. A labyrinth helps direct one's focus toward God. Unlike a maze with dead ends and the possibility of getting lost, a labyrinth has a clear path. Still, it sometimes takes unexpected twists and turns. In this way, it resembles the journey of life.

During my meditative walk, I set an intention to find an answer. I asked God: "What is the next step for me? Am I a musician even though I haven't formally studied music composition?" Am

I supposed to write more songs? I still remember my labyrinth walk clearly. It was a warm autumn day. The sun was shining. It was quiet around me. I was the only person walking the labyrinth that day. I walked slowly and kept asking these questions. When I got to the center, I stood there for some time. I don't remember how long, but at one point, I experienced a wave of emotions. Tears of release and joy ran down my cheeks. I got a clear answer: Write, sing, perform. As I walked out of the labyrinth, I was filled with gratitude.

With that feeling of happiness, I decided to walk through the nearby gardens. During my walk, I received the chorus and first verse of a song that reflected my state of being at that time. By that, I mean the melody and lyrics just came into my mind. I recorded it on my little voice recorder that I started carrying with me to capture ideas or melodies. The best way to explain how a song I am supposed to share comes into my mind is that it feels like a download from a higher power. I am merely a channel.

This is the song that I "downloaded" that day:

The Bigger Picture — © Sabine Kvenberg
Once I realized I was dreaming
In this world that we call our life
Where we play our games with intent
I thought that there must be more than our
    selfish gaining
Of all the stuff that we think we need in this world

I want to live in the bigger picture
I want to keep my vision alive
Want to embrace the earth with healing
Stand in my truth and want to strive
To be the one that I was called to be

Lord, give me strength in my pursuit
I hear the angels singing in me
And I accept this gift from you
I now surrender to your will
And I remember through me you show the way
Show the way

Once I tasted the sweetness of my connection
To unconditional Love and Peace
That is there for us to share
I could not go back to my way of thinking
Now I am awake and know what to do

I want to live in the bigger picture
I want to keep my vision alive
Want to embrace the earth with healing
Stand in my truth and want to strive
To be the one that I was called to be
Lord, give me strength in my pursuit
I hear the angels singing in me
And I accept this gift from you
I now surrender to your will
And I remember through me you show the way
Show the way

The following year, I found myself in Music City, Nashville, to record my first CD. This would not have happened if I had decided not to overcome my fear of sharing my music and message that evening at Unity Village.

Time has passed. Today, I am a public speaker, and I help entrepreneurs become excellent communicators and grow their businesses. I teach them how to craft their Celebrity Signature

Message and present their talks with confidence and poise. I love this part of my life. I keep using my talent and accumulated skills to help others on their journey.

Our lives expand with better communication, growth, and contribution. When we embrace and enjoy the journey of becoming our next greater self, we cannot be anything but happy and grateful for this earthly experience.

To listen to Sabine's songs, visit
https://www.sabinekvenberg.com/music

SABINE KVENBERG, CEO of Impact Communication Coaching, host of the acclaimed BECOME podcast and a best-selling author, is a distinguished Fredericksburg Entrepreneur of the Year dedicated to enhancing the communication prowess of female entrepreneurs. A former actress and director in Europe, Sabine relocated to the US, pioneering a performing arts school that she helmed for over 27 years. Equipped with innovative tools and strategies, Sabine helps entrepreneurs and CEOs master their presentation skills and eradicate the public speaking jitters.

Sabine is on a mission to empower one million entrepreneurs to become excellent communicators so they can share their mission and message to make a positive impact and improve the world by 2028.

Speaking: Your Most Potent Marketing Tool

In the landscape of personal branding, harnessing the power of public speaking is not just an option — it's a necessity. Join Sabine as she reveals how to turn your public speaking skills into a formidable sales tool. To book Sabine for your next event contact her team at Sabine@SabineKvenberg.com.

Connect with Sabine Kvenberg
https://www.sabinekvenberg.com
or scan below for more links

What would you do if all of a sudden you realized that one of the things we take for granted is slowly disappearing? Anne Mok's story will show us that life can be cruel but, at the same time, give us blessings beyond our comprehension. Anne and I first connected on Social Media. I was in the process of writing my TEDx talk as she was waiting to present hers. I was immediately drawn to her bravery but even more to her kindness and sweet demeanor. Her story touched me, and I knew I wanted to include her in this anthology. I was overjoyed when she said yes.

—Sabine Kvenberg

BLIND SIGHTED

by Anne Mok

I slowly and painstakingly started to piece my life back together. Each fragment was a blurred reflection of what I had once been.

CONE ROD DYSTROPHY. Three words would decisively change my vision of the world and how the world would see me.

It was June 2015, a day painted with sunshine outside. I sat in the dimly lit room of my retinal specialist's office. The doctor's lips moved, words spilled out, but it was as though she were speaking a foreign language. A babble of terminology that refused to sink in. I felt numb. Fear, disbelief, and a strange, unsettling relief crashed over me. It was like a nightmare that I couldn't get out of. I asked her to write down those three words — cone-rod dystrophy — not only so I wouldn't forget them but so that I could also understand what this all meant.

I left the appointment and walked quickly to catch the next bus. I had another appointment. This time with HR. A new job, a dream job, had been offered to me. It was a culmination of years of hard work. I was to sign the contract that very day.

Sitting on the bus, I opened my phone to search Dr. Google. It revealed that cone-rod dystrophy was a rare inherited retinal disease that slowly erased the light-sensing cells of my retina. Cones, responsible for color and central vision, were fading first, followed by the rods responsible for night vision and peripheral vision.

There was no cure. Suddenly, the puzzle pieces of my symptoms started to click into place. Questions began to swirl in my head. How much time did I have? What do I do now?

This new job relied on my visual abilities and technical skills. I was torn, confused, and trapped in a time crunch with the added responsibility of providing for my family on a single income. I walked into HR and signed the contract, my heart heavy with uncertainty.

Growing up, I had always struggled with poor vision. By the age of three, I was already wearing glasses. In elementary school, I had those thick coke-bottle lenses. I was terrible at sports. I was always the last kid being picked for teams. It took me years to figure out how to read a clock because we had to look at it on the far wall when I was taught. I couldn't see that there was a minute and a second hand. I also struggled to learn long division because it was conducted on an overhead projector. I couldn't see the far screen, some numbers, or all the steps to solve it.

My other siblings wore glasses, too, so my poor vision was never thoroughly questioned. In 2003, I decided to get laser eye surgery. The transformation was awe-inspiring. The world was suddenly vivid and beautiful. The doctor told me I may still need a small prescription and/or reading glasses when I get older. I fully expected that.

However, in just a few short years, I started sensing that something wasn't *quite right* with my vision. I remember driving my young daughter and me home from a family party one night. It was raining. The drive home was one that I had done so many times and knew so well. I realized I couldn't see the lane lines, the highway signs, or even the plate numbers of the cars in front of me. Anxiety gripped me as I white-knuckled the steering wheel. The night vision was slipping away.

In the daytime, I noticed that I couldn't see the things I *knew* I should be able to see. While driving, I could no longer read the street signs I was all too familiar with. I had trouble catching pedestrians at the edge of my peripheral vision at marked pedestrian crosswalks with no lights. I found that my eyes couldn't adjust to lighting changes, such as from dawn to dusk. These posed the most significant challenges when it came to commuting. I started to become very anxious. I would leave for work early in the morning to beat rush hour traffic, give myself lots of time, and orient myself at work. I would even leave work late to wait until the rush was mostly over.

Perfectionism gripped me as I double-checked my work to compensate for my fading sight. I was known as the focused, diligent, and hardworking employee who noticed even the slightest discrepancies.

At optometrist appointments, I repeated the same sentence, "I'm not seeing what I *know* I'm supposed to see." But, over the years, the tests revealed nothing wrong at each appointment. They did offer me an eyeglass prescription, which was very minimal, and I did fill it out, but my frustration with this unexplained situation began to intensify.

By 2013, I made the painful decision to stop driving. I knew it was the right and only decision. I did not feel safe, and I did not feel comfortable putting my life in danger, especially someone else's. It weighed heavily on my family, burdening my husband, who had suffered a stroke in 2009 and could no longer work. I became the primary breadwinner, juggling two jobs to make ends meet.

I scheduled an appointment with the retinal specialist and explained all my symptoms to her. For the first time, I felt like I was truly listened to. Tearfully, I admitted feeling like I had psychological issues. She looked me straight and said, "I believe you." Tests followed over the next two years, leading to the fateful appointment in June 2015 when I learned of my diagnosis.

Five years of juggling two jobs had culminated in a remarkable opportunity. The part-time job offered me an unattainable position — a substantial salary, exceptional benefits, and a chance to thrive with a fantastic company. There was no way I could say no. I would only need to work one job now. It was better hours, meaning a better quality of life for me to be with my family. It was a much easier transit ride. In June 2015, I signed the contract.

My new job as a nursing assistant in a fertility clinic's procedure room was challenging and fulfilling. I wore my glasses, which helped with my central vision. I adapted through sheer determination. Routine and muscle memory became my allies. I memorized the layout of the room, the placement of the equipment, and the movements of the nurses and doctors. My colleagues viewed me as an exemplary employee, leading accreditation evaluations and training new staff.

I lived a double life. My family knew about my vision loss. My friends struggled to grasp it. My coworkers remained oblivious. I could see, yet I couldn't.

Anxiety gnawed at me, fearing someone would discover my secret at work. My resolve to continue eroded as the years passed. But I had always told myself that when I feel it's time to step away, I will do so.

By the fourth year, I knew it was time to seek assistance from CNIB (Canadian Institute for the Blind). They offered peer support services and initiated my Orientation and Mobility Training on using a white cane, especially on public transit. I carried the cane but hesitated to use it, fearing judgment and misconceptions about blindness. Blindness, I had learned, was a spectrum with varying degrees of visual capability. Not all blind individuals relied on guide dogs or white canes; some wore glasses for protection.

CNIB also helped me navigate the challenging process of requesting accommodations from HR. Honestly, this was something I was utterly terrified of. I was afraid of losing my job. I shed many tears agonizing about this. Discrimination is genuine. Many companies see blind people as a liability. They are hesitant to put accommodations in because they see it as expensive, and there is a lack of understanding.

When I finally approached HR, it was difficult and relieving. I individually informed each of the fertility doctors about my diagnosis. They were all surprised and said that they would never have guessed that I was suffering from any kind of vision loss. The common comment was, "You're the best we've ever had."

In October 2018, I transitioned to a desk position as a Medical Office Assistant. I found it much harder to concentrate and look at the screen for so many hours. I contacted IT to help me make some accommodations on my desktop to make my screen bigger, and my mouse cursor bigger to help me cope.

At this point, only HR, the doctors, the nursing manager, and a couple of very close coworkers knew my "secret." Nobody else knew. I continued to live my double life.

Finally, the end of the year came around, and I was lucky to get off earlier to enjoy the holidays. It was restful. Then, on January 1, 2019, suddenly and without warning, I was struck with a migraine-like headache.

I was diagnosed with NDPH (a new daily persistent headache). It's when a chronic headache begins without warning and lasts 3 months or longer.

The pain mirrors migraines, intensifying with physical activity, light sensitivity, and unpredictable daily fluctuations. It left me unable to complete tasks. I was engulfed in severe depression and bedridden in pain for the first eight months of my diagnosis.

I lost my sense of self. I didn't know who I was, what I liked, or even what I wanted to do. All I felt was pain every moment, every single day.

I still have this headache today as I write this. There is no cure. It is rare and debilitating.

This wasn't the life I wanted or the life I had envisioned. I slowly and painstakingly started to piece my life back together. Each fragment was a blurred reflection of what I had once been. My journey of recovery began with self-acceptance. I needed to accept myself for where I am today and at this moment. With a different perspective, I reflected instead on what I could do.

I could rewrite my story. While bedridden, I saw how the pandemic had magnified the struggles of the visually impaired community and those isolated by chronic illnesses. I also saw the struggle of many small businesses and wanted to find some small way to help.

My Instagram account @purposeinview was created in November 2020. Instagram is a visual medium, and I wanted to challenge its limitations by making it accessible. My mission was to ensure that beauty transcended barriers, reaching every individual while creating an emotional connection. I made the content accessible by providing image descriptions, alt text, audio and video descriptions, and finding a way to make reels more accessible. I was unwavering in my commitment: every audience member should be included.

To support local businesses, I diligently tagged or mentioned them in my Instagram posts. I also included alt text and image descriptions of the products I showcased, extending accessibility to the visually impaired community. Upholding the values of shopping locally and bolstering small businesses became a significant part of my mission. Remarkably, this endeavor became a form of self-care for me. It gave me a profound sense of purpose. Each Instagram post, though labor-intensive for me, structured my days with a clear purpose — getting up to shower, capturing an image, composing a caption, editing, or engaging with my community.

Social media became the gateway to connect with others in the blind and visually impaired community and those with chronic illnesses. These connections helped me to feel less alone and isolated. It also helped to provide a deeper understanding of my own disabilities.

Empathy became a bridge that united us. Sharing experiences fosters understanding and compassion. I was no longer alone in my emotional struggles, despair, hopelessness, and isolation — experiences I still grapple with on my journey with sight loss.

I began to gain an influential presence, securing many collaborations, partnerships, podcasts, speaking engagements, and even a TEDx talk! My devoted community eagerly embraced the unfolding of my vision as I innovatively shared my narrative. They share my values of uplifting others and cheering them on. I have challenged stereotypes, and broken barriers, and shared the lessons from my life to help others relate.

My platform has been the place to bridge the gap between the sighted, blind, and visually impaired community. Many in the sighted community have expressed their willingness and desire to be inclusive and supportive but also need assistance. This opportunity to create conversations of education and awareness has been incredible. I, myself, have had to learn along the way.

My story wouldn't be complete without sharing my experience and giving suggestions on communicating with each other, the sighted and blind or visually impaired community. Below, you will find some helpful pointers that will make it more comfortable to interact with someone who is blind or visually impaired:

When you see someone with a white cane or a guide dog, respect their independence and personal space. Just because they have a visual impairment does not mean they need constant assistance, as they may have their own strategies for navigating the environment.

If they need help or clarification, introduce yourself and ask if they would like assistance. If they decline, respect that they know best and move on.

Use clear and descriptive language. For example, instead of saying "over there," you can say, "Three steps ahead, to your left." There is also no need to talk loudly or slowly.

Don't honk, yell, or wave to a pedestrian with a white cane or guide dog. It is very startling and unsafe. Many blind people are trained to listen to the traffic and wait until it has stopped.

Guide dogs are working hard to help their handlers.

Sometimes, we can't help but want to pet and become best friends with the guide dogs we meet, but that's only sometimes appropriate. When a guide dog is wearing its harness, it means "hands off" and that it is working.

Living with the constant presence of new daily persistent headaches has taught me to focus on those moments of low pain, foster my resilience, and solidify the values that hold the most meaning to me. It has empowered me to tap into my inner strength and determination. In those times of pain that forced me into darkness, it is then that I've chosen to focus on moments of creativity. It's extraordinary that my creative spark ignites out of those darkest hours.

Vision loss, in its own way, has been a gift of revelation for me. It has opened doors, expanded my thinking horizons, allowed me to be who I was meant to be, and allowed me to see the world through a different lens. Most importantly, it whispered to me that everything would be okay despite all odds.

My Purpose In View
My vision loss is a journey
Although genetic in nature
And an outcome of some level of blindness,
I am the author of my own narrative.
I can change my own perspective
To aspire to find my purpose in view.
The opposite of blindness is view.

ANNE MOK, a fearless advocate, TEDx speaker, and blind storyteller, reshapes the narrative of a purposeful life, defying odds with resilience and determination. Her inspiring journey is a beacon of hope, navigating life's challenges with unwavering courage. Committed to making a positive impact, Anne illuminates lives, demonstrating that greatness knows no boundaries.

Reflecting on her journey, Anne embraces her blindness and Asian heritage to rewrite her life's path. She inspires others to embrace their unique stories and voices. Anne forges connections and fosters inclusivity, overcoming barriers with remarkable ability.

Active on social media, Anne leverages her influence to bring education and awareness to the blind community, advocating for their rights. She creates a space for dialogue and change, empowering individuals and contributing to a more inclusive society.

Anne's story is one of triumph, resilience, and the transformative power of embracing identity, leaving an indelible mark on the world. Her ongoing advocacy inspires, educates, and promotes a more inclusive and understanding society.

Connect with Anne Mok
https://purposeinview.com
https://www.instagram.com/purposeinview

I first met Monica at a girls' game night playing Rommikub. We had so much fun together. Little did I know that her past was so hard and turbulent that it could qualify for a movie drama. A friend who knew I was gathering stories for my book said: "Talk to Monica, she has a story to tell." Boy, my friend was right. Monica's experiences are one of those many women would not want to share out of fear or shame. Monica was different. She wanted to tell her story and, in the end, was able to release the past.

—Sabine Kvenberg

HEALING HEARTS, FINDING LOVE

by Monica Retchin

I worked so hard with all my therapists to heal myself, to find the Monica that was buried inside, the person I wanted to be so badly.

IT WAS A beautiful day sitting on the passenger seat of our Range Rover with my King Charles Cavalier on my lap. My husband of 30 years was driving the car back from what was supposed to be a relaxing, wonderful summer in our Tennessee mountain log cabin when I finally realized... I CAN'T DO THIS ONE MORE DAY!!!

I was dreading the 14-hour drive before it even began, and when he started blaming me for his unhappiness and giving me the look I disliked so much, something inside me happened. I started asking him all the questions I wanted answers to, specifically about our daughter's eating disorder. She was 18 when she developed anorexia, and I remember that time as one of my most challenging moments in life. While she was at Remuda Ranch in Arizona, a remarkable healing program, they asked her to draw her family. and in that drawing, she pulled her father as a tornado spitting fire at her as a dying flower. It was such a perfect description it made my hair stand up. So, I asked him. Do you take any responsibility for our daughter's eating disorder? He looked at me and said ABSOLUTELY NOT!!! That was your enmeshment with her.

At that moment, a light bulb went off, and I knew I had to be done!!!! There was no way I could stay married to this man. I had already spent 30 years of my life scared, tip-toeing around, always waiting for the next explosion, never being able to live in the moment, and being blamed for everything.

So when I got home, we met with our daughters, who were 23 and 26 at the time. They, of course, were not surprised at all. Both girls tried explaining to their dad that living with him was difficult, but he blamed me. I got up very calmly, walked upstairs into my closet, grabbed the suitcase, and threw some clothing in. I walked out, got in my car, left the home I had lived in for 20 years, and never returned. It was the only way I could do it. I left my beautiful home, my doggy, and everything behind.

I checked into a hotel about 12 miles away. It was dark by the time I arrived. I remember showering and collapsing in bed. I didn't even cry. I think I was in shock. However, I never looked back or doubted myself once I made that decision. And for sure, now, 11 years later, it was the most significant, most difficult, but best decision I've ever made.

I was busy the next week finding a place to move into. I found a beautiful place with a bay view where I could see the sunrise. The minute I stepped into that apartment, I felt at home. Decorating and shopping kept me busy, but my mood changed when the holidays approached. I definitely was not prepared for all the pain I was getting ready to experience. It's sad when I think back to that time how naive I was to believe that walking away from a 30-year marriage would be easy once I had the strength to do it. I was a lost, damaged soul, alone and hiding.

I no longer knew who I was or what I wanted in life. I joined a gym, which I have always loved to work out at, and started meeting a few new girls. I would spend my nights alone drinking white wine, feeling really sorry for myself, hating what I was doing, but having no clue how to fix myself!

My daughters have always been my dearest friends and company, but I now realize they also suffered in their own way. My ex decided to announce that he had left me because I was an alcoholic, and because I had left the house, it was easy for people to believe him...... he would even warn the girls to be careful when they were with me because I was dangerous.

One afternoon, I was with my oldest daughter and her 2 boys when I overheard him say that on the phone, and she did not defend me.….. I ran out of her house in tears; my heart ached like I had never ached before.

My ex is a controlling narcissist and could have never lived with everyone, knowing it was me who left him. His last words to me before I left the house were: YOU WON'T LAST A DAY WITHOUT ME!!!! I have dedicated my life to my daughters, always there for them in every school activity and every big and small step while growing up. I often felt guilty that I had given them the father they had, a man who loved them in his way as long as they didn't bother or upset him. A man who would walk into the house after a day at work and lose it for any little thing. We lived waiting and trying to minimize his explosions. It was so bad that the girls were 9 and 6 when they made signs for the door from the garage to the house that said CALM DOWN, DADDY.

I was a total mess when the holidays arrived a few months after I left. Resentments were piling up. My loneliness was through the roof, and my wine drinking escalated to a bottle a night. I was in disbelief at how easily you could be forgotten by your neighbors and your ex's family members, who had been part of your life for 30 years.

My ex had a woman in his bed already. I had been replaced in the blink of an eye. I thought this should not hurt like it is hurting. I'm the one who wanted the divorce, but I couldn't deny my feelings. I was in a black hole. The only thing I remember about that holiday time is crying a lot and having to see my ex at my daughter's house for Christmas. Thank God for my 2 beautiful grandboys who brought so much joy to my life.

Life went on for a few years. I dreaded holidays because I hated my ex and did not want to see him. My youngest daughter started dating a handsome man from Louisiana, and a couple of years into the relationship, she moved there. I was thrilled for her as I really liked him.

One evening, I saw pictures on Facebook of the two of them with your ex and his new woman celebrating at a restaurant. My heart sank so hard...... I started crying like a baby. I felt so stepped on like no one cared about my feelings..... how can my daughter be getting engaged and have planned this with her father, and I know absolutely nothing about it?

Needless to say, that night, a bottle of wine was not enough. The next day, I did not take her calls. When we finally talked, she kept saying it was all planned between her fiancée and her dad, and she knew nothing about it. My future son-in-law went down a few pegs in my heart, but knowing how controlling my ex is, I knew it had been him who, when he asked for our daughter's hand, had made all the arrangements.

Planning her wedding was a mixture of feelings, happiness, and either fear or anxiety. I was indeed a woman filled with resentment and, yes, hatred. All these ugly feelings filled my heart with a few joyful moments when I spent time with my grandsons, or I was traveling where I could pretend I was whole and not broken.

The day of her bridal shower, which I had planned with so much love and looked forward to for many months, was a disaster. I was super anxious as my ex's sisters, whom I had not seen in years, were on the guest list. Also invited was his new wife. When my daughter proceeds to tell me dad is coming to the bridal shower my heart started pounding out of control. I started shaking and said absolutely not. He is not invited. And she said he would stay at the bar downstairs to say hi to me. I could not believe my ears; this man does whatever he wants. He tramples over everybody's feelings and thinks he can waltz into her party.

While I was getting ready, I was so out of control I decided to take a Xanax to calm my nerves was the biggest mistake I could have made. Little did I know that this night would change my life forever.

We arrived at the beautiful outdoor restaurant. The place looked beautiful, even though it was very hot and the fans blew cold air. It was a perfect evening. I introduced myself to the staff, and they started pouring the wine. As all the guests were arriving, my anxiety started building up. I'm not sure how many glasses I had, but for certain, too many.

As the night went on, I realized I was not in a good place. I walked over to one of my daughter's best friends and questioned her about talking to my ex's new wife; it made her feel very uncomfortable, so she went and told my daughter. My daughter confronted me, saying, Mom, what are you doing? I don't remember anything that happened after that, but I've been told I gave her the finger and started fighting with her. I do remember seeing her crying, and that made me even madder. I left and drove home in that condition. God was with me because I made it home with no problem.

The next day, I woke up nauseous and with a headache. The minute I opened my eyes, my heart sank deeper than ever been. I rushed out of bed to see if my daughter was still there, but she and her fiancé were gone. They were leaving my place at 6 am and going back to Louisiana. No note, no, I love you mom like she always left me, or I hate you mom for what you did. I had ruined her bridal shower. Not only that, now everyone had proof that what my ex said about me being drunk was true. Monica is an alcoholic.

This was the one and only time I felt like I wanted to be dead. I wished I could redo the night, knowing it was impossible. I kept pacing my apartment like a crazy person, so embarrassed to pick up the phone and call someone for help.

I grabbed a calendar and marked all the days till my birthday, 42 days till I turned 60. I had sent invites for a luncheon with girl-friends, but I said to myself I won't have a drink till then, but when the evening came, all the good intentions were out the window. I was all alone, the guilt I felt was so overwhelming, the hatred I felt in my heart was so intense I couldn't take it any longer, so I turned to my friend, the wine bottle. I realized then how sick, lonely, and broken I was. I had hurt what I loved the most in my life: my daughters!!!! I had hit rock bottom. That's when I realized I needed help beyond anything I had done before.

The next day, I checked myself into a safe haven place for 30 days to try to find myself. It was an act of desperation, but that's precisely how I felt that morning.

They sent a car to pick me up. Once I sat in it, I started crying like a baby. I wanted to go back to my apartment, to my bed, bury myself under the sheets, and never come out again. I can't even put words to it because nothing would be awful enough to describe it. The ride took 2 hours, and when the welcoming committee greeted me, I was so exhausted; all I wanted was a bed and to sleep for days, which is precisely what I did.

Those 30 days were the most life-changing days of my life; I realized how full of resentment I was. Not only did I resent my ex, but I also resented my daughters for not defending me against the awful things their dad said about me; I resented my father for my sad childhood and more people that aren't even worth mentioning.

I worked so hard with all my therapists to heal myself, to find the Monica that was buried inside, the person I wanted to be so badly.

While I was there, I met a man who caught my attention. We had lots in common and yet very different upbringings and lives. Talking with him in the evenings made my stay pleasant, much more than I ever imagined it could be. I had such a positive experience and learned so much about myself and people in general that when I left the facility, I was ready to face the world again. Jeffrey, the man I met, was my partner at my daughter's wedding and helped me stand on my own two feet. We had a wonderful time, and more importantly, my daughter had an evening she will never forget. All wonderful memories!

It has been 4 years since I became impatient, and I can tell you I am totally different. I have grown emotionally and spiritually. I live in peace. I am happy and for the first time in my life. I no longer feel like I can't have a good day if one of my daughters is having trouble. I acknowledge it, give advice, reaffirm my love for them, and know it is not my place to solve their problems. I know how important communication is, that I can have my thoughts, beliefs, and most of all, my own words!

I live a life I never even imagined. Jeffrey, my fiancé now, loves me like I am, from head to toe! We have a loving dog named Aspen. I walk the beach and swim almost daily, and I never forget to say THANK YOU, GOD!

Thank you, Jeffrey; you have shown me real happiness, peace, and life I only dreamed of. I now live in the moment, love life, and can not wait for what God has in store for us. And to my beautiful mom, hope you are smiling in heaven, looking down and seeing how truly happy I am as you were the only person who knew my real unhappiness in my marriage.

Writing my story has been very painful. I have shed many tears but have healed more in the process. It has also made me so grateful for where I am now.

My friend, if you are reading my story and you are in pain or are in an abusive relationship, know that there is life after that. Life is not supposed to be like that! It takes work, but it is so worth it. Life is beautiful, and I could have never said that before.

MONICA RETCHIN, originally from Lima, Peru, embarked on a life journey that has been nothing short of remarkable. In 1973, at the tender age of 13, Monica and her parents, two brothers, and two sisters made the life-altering move to Miami. Her pursuit of knowledge led her to institutions like Miami Dade and Florida International University, where she dedicated herself to studying accounting and marketing, laying the foundation for a successful career. Monica played a pivotal role in building a highly prosperous medical business alongside her ex-husband for a quarter of a century. Their dedication paid off when Humana Health Insurance acquired their business in 2012.

Monica is a proud mother of two beautiful daughters and the doting grandmother of four amazing grandsons, cherishing every moment she spends with her family. She now resides in the picturesque Siesta Key, Sarasota, where she lives her dream life alongside her fiancé and their adorable golden doodle, Aspen.

Connect with Monica Retchin
mretchin30@gmail.com

Laura and I met when working in a program with Tony Robins and Dean Graziosi. Later, she joined my mastermind group. Little did I know that this connection formed our friendship to this day. Laura is a strong, fun woman who has the biggest smile. If you are with her, you can't do anything but feel good and laugh together. Her strength and outlook on life were tested when she wanted to become a mother.

— Sabine Kvenberg

RESILIENT LIFE: FLIPPING GRIT AND GRACE TO MOTHERHOOD

by Laura Mak Quist

Fitness, my lifetime constant companion, helped me reclaim control of my body lovingly. I gently began to feel the rush of life's force coursing through once lethargic limbs, now getting a flow of blood into my muscles, awakening them again.

AS SOON AS my husband placed our son gently on my chest, and I felt his warmth and fragility against my skin, the universe stopped for a moment. Celebrating our victory over adversity, each heartbeat echoed the memories of our struggles. But the significance of that moment made all the obstacles we faced shine with a profound purpose. Our hearts danced with the rhythm of a new start, a journey taken and conquered, a love that had grown strong through life's trials into this beautiful moment of fulfillment.

I never experienced the whimsical depiction of "pregnancy bliss" that society often romanticizes. Instead, my story was filled with challenges that tested our determination at every corner. The idealized visions of pregnancy were exchanged for a reality check that came without warning. Our son's entry into this world was far from typical. Yet, every thump of his heart demonstrated the infinite bravery that propelled our journey.

Life had weaved its story in a highly unusual way. My husband and I met later in life. Our love grew over the months we dated, and it was clear that we wanted to tie the knot and start a family. At our engagement party, we shared with our friends the thought of a beach wedding, and much to our surprise, we had over 30 yes' for attendees! We had a small family and chose a family-only wedding in California. My dad walked me down the aisle like I had always dreamed about. He sat next to me quietly for a few moments. In a quiet and calm voice, unlike his typical boisterous and jolly tone, he shared my favorite quote from the day with me. "Best day of my life," he said in a proudly confident manner as he bowed his head to accept the blessing of the day.

The following day, our group headed to Fiji for a week with 34 of our dear friends. On Day 6, we exchanged vows on the pristine sands of Fiji. I was escorted down the aisle lined with tropical flowers and pink and orange ribbons (my favorite "happy" colors), with my loving Fijian Warriors to guide the way. I met my husband under the floral arch, with the waves crashing in the background and the sun gently shining, creating a moment we forever remember.

It was barely six months later when I received a phone call from my brother in the middle of the night. Half asleep, I answered the phone. My brother's voice was sad and quiet. I instinctively knew that something was wrong. He gave me the heartbreaking news that my father lost his longtime battle with cancer.

Consequently, his death cast a shadow, but within that sadness, our desire for parenthood only grew. Time, with its relentless pace, seemed to be in a race with our dreams. Yet, my unyielding belief stemmed from a lifetime of nurturing a body and soul that defied age, a mind that soared beyond the ordinary, and a spirit that danced to the tunes of hope. The mirror reflected an exterior untouched by time, and I had a quaint belief that the youthfulness I felt outside was mirrored within.

We faced challenges at every turn but persevered with great courage and self-advocacy. The unconventional path we took demanded bravery and fortitude with every step. Our story isn't about conforming to society's norms but about believing in ourselves and taking charge of our lives where possible.

My biological clock was ticking, even though I felt and looked much younger than I was. However, by this time, I knew I didn't want to take chances of missing the boat to parenthood. So it began, I was determined to use those virtues ingrained through a lifetime of athletic discipline to keep me moving forward on this journey — tenacity, coachability, and a relentless quest to venture beyond the conventional.

We started at the beginning. I was ready to be the most "coach-able" client this clinic had ever had. I can follow the directions to a "T," and the desired results should happen, right? Ha! This journey was just about to enlighten me in ways I could not have imagined.

I was never one to be "too squeamish" at needles, but to be fair, I never cared for them. Following the precise directions of "inject in a dart-like motion," our IVF journey seemed to be coming. Five shots a day for about 10 days or so. The anxiety lessened slightly, I suppose, but was always present. Only a prayer and faith seemed to soothe me.

The number of hurdles a woman must clear before becoming pregnant through IVF is vast and much like that of a gymnast on a quest for Gold at the Olympics. Each step was like qualifying for the next round. She competes at various levels, nationally and internationally. Then, if she is lucky enough to peak in the right 4th year, the one with the Olympics, she may be selected to be part of the team. Each competition brings her closer to that dream. I discovered that my IVF journey had many intricate steps, even before getting pregnant. My gymnastics quest taught me a lot about persistence and perseverance. Our journey is not always a straight path. Even though I never made the Olympic team, I had a better one; my Olympic-like Gold was finally earned once we created our family.

In my case, as a "high risk" candidate (because of my whopping age of 40 years old), I had to be on bed rest for the following two weeks after the transfer. As a collegiate gymnast and retired professional athlete, being sedentary was one of the hardest parts!

I did not get pregnant on our first round. The extreme amount of emotional devastation for both my husband and I was just the beginning of a roller coaster ride of emotions. Our mental health was challenged in a way like never before.

However, I did get pregnant on our second round. Our son's embryo was transferred one year later to the exact day my dad passed away. That will forever be a date we will remember.

As I mentioned earlier, pregnancy bliss did not make it to me. I had nausea for about eight and a half months of the journey. For basically the first two weeks, I felt "ok", just the mental ping pong of thoughts swirling through my head of whether this will work and what if it doesn't work. Then there was always this lingering sensation of queasiness and, if I wasn't careful, full-on nausea. I exercised during the entire pregnancy, which often helped with the nausea. My intensity was tremendously different as I was still a "high risk" label. Even though I worked out and ate healthy, nourishing foods for "Baby Q," I gained an astounding 65 pounds!

About seven months after my delivery, I was able to drop the pregnancy weight, begin sleeping a few more consecutive hours, and stop breastfeeding so we could start trying for a sibling. This was when more health scares began. There was an issue with my thyroid levels that quickly led to a diagnosis of Hashimoto's disease. It is an autoimmune disease where the body is tricked into attacking the organs and cells. This can happen for some women after breastfeeding finishes. This disease traditionally needs to be treated with medications. We learned we could not even begin to start trying to get pregnant until my thyroid was in a healthy range. In the beginning, I just thought that medication was the only way to go. But as I continued to research and invest time in other practices, I learned more about what other protocols could help me.

Cheers to getting my thyroid within a healthy range so we can try for a sibling for our son. We tried not once, not twice, but a third time. They say, "The third time's a charm", but the journey was far from charming. Although I got pregnant, the unsurmountable number of emotions during this period was breathtaking. The challenge of these losses along the way, the excessive amounts of hormones pumped into my body, and the tornado of emotions that swirled around almost fully exhausted us. I like to say I am surrounded by my "happy bubble," but the bubble kept getting poked and prodded during this time. Only by sheer willpower and prayer did my bubble not pop!

We made it to the twelve-week window and then got the news. There was something wrong with the baby. For the next seven weeks, we kept getting more testing done to learn and wrap our heads around what was happening. The doctor used the analogy of how rare this is by comparing it to finding the single letter typo in a paragraph, of a chapter, from a novel, in a trilogy, found in one of the largest libraries somewhere in all the world. Nothing was ever more abrupt and devastating at the same time as learning that our baby may not make it, then just a few days later, losing him.

Just like that, a late-term pregnancy loss shattered our world.

Oh, how the heart quivers at the prospect of diving back into life's turbulent waters after being tossed ashore in a tiny, fragile boat. The tale of that year, post the shattering loss, is one of gritty resilience, tender mercies, and the gentle rekindling of hope in the sorrow-laden mists.

When the fabric of our existence was torn apart by that late-term pregnancy loss, it felt as though the heavens themselves wept with us. The world became a haze of tears and heartache; every breath seemed to echo the emptiness. Yet amid the shattering silence, there emerged a rhythm of survival, a hum of enduring love that pulsed through the veins of our little family. It was our toddler son, his eyes brimming with the untouched innocence and wonder of life. His everyday giggle for life and zest for outdoor walks to meet new puppies was a gentle reminder of life's enduring beauty and the treasures we still held close.

Faith, our strong anchor, held us steady as the waves of despair fought to sweep us away. Our family shared their love and also grieved with us. We were also blessed with wonderful warrior friends who kept us afloat with supportive words and comforting gestures like healthy prepared meals, quality time, silent walks, or frivolous topics of conversation to take me away from my harsh reality.

Fitness, my lifetime constant companion, helped me reclaim control of my body lovingly. I gently began to feel the rush of life's force coursing through once lethargic limbs, now getting a flow of blood into my muscles, awakening them again. I became re-acquainted with my yoga mat, connected more with nature on our walks, and gradually gained enough strength to lift weights. All of these movements complimented my healing journey so I could gain confidence in myself as a woman, mom, wife, and friend.

When I started fading into an unsavory mindset, I became mindful of my surroundings, seeking every small joy I could find. Each sunset that painted the sky promised a sunrise, a fresh canvas of 24 hours where healing could inch forward, where joy could tiptoe back into my heart. The camaraderie of nature was soothing; the parks became my refuge; each tree seemed to stand tall in solidarity, and each blossom seemed to whisper hope. Gradually, it appeared to nuzzle away a tiny fraction of my grief.

The days rolled on, morphing into a tapestry of healing moments. At last, the sweet epiphany dawned; we were ready to invite another soul into our family, to offer our hearts again on the altar of life. And oh, the joy only after a second round of IVF, post loss, when life bloomed once more! The universe hummed a lullaby as we welcomed our second son, a testament to life's grace and the enduring strength of hope.

My chapter of self-recovery began now that we have completed our family. I knew I needed to become my fullest, healthiest, and energetic self to be the best mom to these two boys that we adored beyond our words.

At 44 years old, I began my quest to heal from Hashimotos, drop the second 60 pounds of baby weight, and just strengthen my "mom of two" body and mind. I sought to untangle the mystery of my health, mend what was broken, and restore the lost balance. Hashimoto's was not merely a diagnosis; it was a terrain to navigate, a challenge to meet eye to eye. Traditional medicine offered its aid, but deep in my heart, I knew there was more. I was ready to begin a comprehensive healing that danced to the rhythm of nature, too.

And so began my exploration into unconventional healing. Acupuncture, steeped in ancient wisdom, called out to me, promising to unlock my inner vitality. I embarked on a five-year journey with a skilled acupuncturist, tailoring each session to address my needs. Initially, we focused on nurturing my thyroid, dedicating eight months to weekly treatments.

Yoga, a longtime companion, took on a new role in supporting my weary thyroid. It offered a gentle path to better health through poses and mindful breathing. I delved deeper, studying yoga therapy for thyroid healing. These classes encompassed calming breathwork, stimulating chants, nurturing postures, and visualization meditations. I still enjoy practicing many of these to this day.

Nutrition also played a vital role in my holistic well-being journey. It wasn't just about satisfying hunger but inviting vitality, balance, and cellular harmony. My diet included essential foods like Brazil nuts, lightly cooked leafy greens, healthy fats, salmon, fresh fruits, and berries. I embraced an anti-inflammatory meal plan, incorporating spices such as turmeric, ginger, and garlic.

Self-advocacy became my guiding star on this voyage. I became a passionate researcher, inquisitive experimenter, and devoted caregiver to my body. The fusion of Eastern wisdom and Western science paved a path for my healing. It eventually led to a momentous decision. Two years later, I inquired with my doctor about discontinuing thyroid medication, and she agreed, with the provision to resume if necessary. Six years have passed, and my thyroid hormones remain within a healthy range, free from daily medication.

It was a graceful dance, an attunement to my body's whispers, a tribute to its needs, and a celebration of its progress. I didn't combat my health issues but embraced them with love, understanding, and a touch of playful curiosity. This journey stands as a testament to the power of exploring unconventional paths, becoming advocates for our well-being, and embracing diverse approaches to healing.

It has been a remarkable odyssey, painted with the hues of pain, love, hope, and the sweet victory of self-discovery! This narrative aims to reach the hearts of those navigating similar challenges, offering a beacon of hope and a resilient melody that resonates through the darkest moments, urging the spirit to keep dancing to life's rhythm.

Meet **LAURA MAK QUIST**, the radiant force behind Women's Wellness coaching and an inspiring speaker. With a journey as remarkable as her achievements, she's a former NCAA Collegiate scholarship gymnast turned master trainer, former professional athlete, international yoga instructor, and retreat leader with 30 years of experience in the fitness industry.

Laura Mak is the embodiment of 'wisely fierce,' a term she coined to describe a woman in tune with her body, who embraces mindful living, is open to growth, and is always learning.

As a dedicated advocate for women over 40, Laura empowers them to elevate their health, work productivity, and businesses. She's a guiding light, offering insights on business growth, mindful living, visualization, and the importance of adding meditation to one's life.

Join Laura Mak on her path as she is a sought-after speaker who is ready to inspire and motivate women at conferences, women's events, and business groups. Her infectious energy, wisdom, and 'wisely fierce' spirit are sure to leave you invigorated.

Connect with Laura Mak
https://www.LauraMakFitLife.com
https://www.Instagram.com/LauraMakFitLife

We both grew up in Germany but met here in the US, where we now live. I met Bianca at a networking event. It is always great to speak your native language occasionally and connect with someone who shares similar memories of a country you grew up in. Of course, when I heard Bianca's story, I asked her to share it here. Oftentimes, I have been asked how it was to leave my country and start all over again somewhere else. Bianca shares her journey, leaving behind everything she built to start anew.

— *Sabine Kvenberg*

FINDING THE NEW ME... THE AMERICAN WAY

by Bianca Bendraouia

Saying goodbye to the place I called home was hard, and starting over in a new country was both scary and exciting. It felt like I was weaving together the memories of my past with the colors of my new life.

I STILL VIVIDLY remember the days leading up to the closure of my yarn store, "Wollig Warm & Kleine Schätze," in Germany in 2015. The decision to move to America had been both exciting and heartbreaking. My husband and I were living in a long-distance marriage. For years, my husband's work had him travel overseas. Sometimes, it kept us apart for months at a time. My son was 11, and I felt he needed his father more than ever. As a family, we decided it was time to make that move.

My shop was more than just a place to sell yarn. It was where people who loved knitting came together to share stories and laughter. The colorful shelves filled with yarn showed how much I loved running my little "Lädle". The people who entered the store were more than customers; they were friends and, in some cases, family.

When I told everyone about closing, they showed up in large numbers. Friends and customers came to say goodbye, sharing hugs and memories. They told me how important the shop had been for them during hard times. The days before closing were emotional. Packing away the yarn made me remember all our good times in the shop. They were as colorful as the wool that lined the shelves. On the last day, there were tears and laughter. People gave me handmade gifts, letters, and well wishes.

Closing the shop was sad. Standing outside, I cried as I said goodbye. The memories made in Wollig Warm & Kleine Schätze will always stay with me. But as I left, holding my memories close to my heart, I knew that even though the shop was closing, the friendships and love from my German community would stay with me. They would always be a part of my life, no matter where I went, including my new adventure in America.

We stood in line to get through the security with our one-way ticket. It was a weary feeling to leave my home behind to start all over again in a new country, thousands of miles away from everything I ever knew. After a long flight, we arrived in the land of opportunities.

Leaving Germany for the USA was like riding a roller coaster of feelings. Saying goodbye to the place I called home was hard, and starting over in a new country was both scary and exciting. It felt like I was weaving together the memories of my past with the colors of my new life.

As I settled into my new life in the USA, my memories returned to my beloved yarn store. Leaving behind my business in Germany felt like closing a chapter of my life. The prospect of beginning anew in a foreign country was thrilling and intimidating. I had boxes of colorful yarn from my previous business, but I knew that starting another yarn store wasn't the path I wanted to take. It was time to explore new passions.

When our best friends from Germany came to visit, we all went on a trip to Key West, and that journey changed everything for me. We laughed a lot and shared many good times. My friend, who has been taking photos for decades, and I had a little photo contest during our trip. Who is going to take THE best photo? I loved challenges and competitions. On one of our days in Key West, we went into an art gallery showcasing the amazing photos of Peter Lik. His pictures of nature were so beautiful that I couldn't look away. It brought out feelings in me that I hadn't felt in a while. Looking at those pictures made me want to learn how to capture moments like that. When looking back, I laugh at myself. It is not easy to take those breathtaking pictures. You have to know your craft.

So, I decided to give photography a try. I read books, watched videos, and practiced a lot. At first, I took pictures of landscapes like

Lik, but soon, I discovered that I enjoyed taking pictures of people more. I loved capturing their feelings and stories through my camera.

Learning about photography during this time felt like finding a cozy spot for my heart. It made me happy, and it let me capture a bunch of different feelings. It was like holding a magic tool that could keep moments from slipping away. Taking pictures wasn't just about clicking buttons. It was about understanding people's feelings and the cool stories their faces told. With my camera, I could show more than just smiles – I could capture what made each person special.

Being behind the camera was like finding peace. It let me express myself without using words, like a painter using colors on a canvas. The camera was my way of showing the world's beauty and how life is sometimes delicate. When the camera clicked, it felt like a heartbeat. It wasn't just a sound; it was like music made of feelings, telling stories with every picture. Through the camera lens, I could peek into people's hearts and learn about their stories with every snap.

In this sea of emotions, photography turned into more than a hobby. It became something important to who I am. The camera wasn't just a thing; it was like a part of me, helping me share the amazing and complicated things in the world. Every picture was like a brushstroke, creating a painting full of emotions that showed the dance of life.

As I got deeper into photography, it became more than just a skill. It became a big part of who I am. The camera wasn't just a tool; it was like a bridge connecting my feelings to the world. So, in every picture, I found not just happiness but a strong link to the beautiful mix of emotions life has to offer – a connection that spoke louder than words.

This new adventure, filled with surprises and changes, was a beautiful ride I never expected when I closed my yarn store in Germany.

Over time, my newfound love for portrait photography evolved into a flourishing business. I began offering my services to capture the essence of individuals and families through the camera lens. With each click, I found joy in revealing the beauty and uniqueness of every person I photographed.

As the years passed, I reflected on the journey that had brought me to this moment. While I had left behind my beloved yarn store and the memories associated with it, I had discovered a new purpose and a thriving business that brought happiness to my heart.

The transition from Germany to the USA was challenging, but it opened doors to unexpected opportunities and allowed me to embrace my true passion. In the end, the threads of my life had unraveled and woven a new tapestry in America, one filled with vibrant colors and the smiles of the people I had the privilege to photograph. The memories of my yarn store remained a cherished part of my past, but the future holds endless possibilities and adventures in my newfound world of photography.

BIANCA BENDRAOUIA. In the colorful chapters of her life, Bianca began her entrepreneurial journey at a young age, transitioning from owning a yarn store in Germany to proudly steering a flourishing photography business in the United States. Closing the doors to her initial venture in 2015 marked the commencement of an exciting new chapter. Fueled by a deep passion for storytelling, she ventured into photography, skillfully transforming ordinary moments into enduring memories.

A wife and mother, she successfully juggled family life while building a photography business from scratch. Her achievement demanded a keen eye for capturing emotions and unwavering dedication to mastering the craft. Through hard work and resilience, Bianca turned her early dreams into a thriving enterprise. Join her on this visual journey, where each photo isn't just an image but a stroke in the canvas of her entrepreneurial story—a testament to the remarkable possibilities that unfold when passion aligns with purpose.

Connect with Bianca Bendraouia
www.biancabenphotography.com
www.boudoirbybiancaben.com

Through the podcast community, I met Anna. She has an inspiring podcast called In Turn. Anna's story by itself is inspiring. It shows us that no matter where we start in life, there is always room for growth. Her story gives us hope and guidelines for improving our lives as well. Her story of loss started the process of finding herself.
— Sabine Kvenberg

MY QUEST: DISCOVERING THE LIFE I WAS MEANT TO LIVE

by Anna Brook

You build your inner strength and resilience when you choose not to give up on your dreams and keep moving forward.

IT WAS JANUARY 11, 2018, a day like any other, so I thought. The alarm finally went off and woke me up as usual. I opened my eyes but was still half asleep. Another day of work. It was cold, dark, and quiet outside, so I had to force myself to get ready. After getting out of the shower, I still had time to enjoy my morning coffee. As soon as I took a sip, I heard a text notification on my phone. Who may be texting me that early in the morning? It was my mother. I knew something happened since it was unlike her to text me at that hour. Besides, she would instead call and talk. Suddenly, my mind started racing and worrying. I felt like I became paralyzed when I saw the text. She wrote that my younger brother passed away that night at the age of 21. I couldn't believe it was real. Suddenly, I remembered him being born and how I cared for him growing up as a big sister and a friend. How can a life end at 21? He didn't even have a chance to live fully. I couldn't accept that this was happening.

The sudden death of my brother brought up a lot of unsettling emotions in me, such as grief, sadness, and anxiety. Mainly because I was going through a divorce at the same time. I didn't know how to process the emotional intensity I was feeling. I was never taught that in my life. Quite the opposite, showing emotions in my family was never welcomed, and I learned how to suppress them. I was in a dark mental place. It was so hard for me to talk to anyone, even to my friends and family, since I truly believed that people would judge me for choosing to file for divorce. I thought that my decision to finally choose myself would look selfish and inconsiderate in the eyes of others, to the point where I convinced myself that people would reject having me as a friend.

Feeling isolated and abandoned, I found escape in working a lot and keeping my mind off thinking about anything that would trigger unpleasant emotions I had to deal with.

After putting myself through so much stress mentally and physically, I ended up being in the hospital. That's when I first experienced a panic attack and was in the worst pain ever. I was scared that I might die, and no one would ever know about that until later. I felt extremely depressed and lonely. So, I started questioning myself: Was my life mine by choice? Or perhaps there is more to life for me that would bring me happiness, joy, love, and fulfillment. I had a deep understanding or intuition that something was not right, not how it was supposed to be, and definitely not how I should be feeling.

Even though I spent most of my life studying and chasing different educational degrees to prove my self-worth, I felt like an imposter, as if I did not know enough or was not capable enough to make essential decisions in life, such as making certain career moves or establishing my own business. Moreover, I was constantly worried about others' opinions, feeling judged and critical of myself. I believed that to start something new, I had to have more knowledge, know the right people, and have a perfect plan that would always succeed. I always considered myself a perfectionist. I was scared even to see that it might work because I would picture the worst-case scenario of a possible outcome based on other people's stories of failures. In addition, I listened to those who were not successful in their lives. I also needed proper boundaries to teach people how I wanted to be treated. In other words, I was disconnected from my truth and conditioned not to speak up on what was important.

At the time, I didn't value myself enough to believe I could live my dream life and have everything I desired. As a result, I worked crazy hours as a pharmacist, did not spend enough time with my son and my loved ones, and did not genuinely enjoy my life. I escaped the present moment by working a lot. Working was my way to avoid dealing with unpleasant emotions that would occasionally come to the surface. I was constantly suppressing them since I considered it a sign of weakness to let myself feel. So, I started to distract myself from facing unpleasant emotions with different coping behaviors like not engaging in deep conversations on purpose, remaining reserved, and pleasing people to prevent confrontation.

On top of that, I kept everything to myself since I thought no one would understand what I was going through. With those beliefs in place, I was suffering in silence, not knowing that I was the one doing that to myself in the first place. Also, I have been raised to believe that working hard is the only way to earn money and that making a lot of money is impossible without making sacrifices, like giving up free time to spend with my family and friends or to travel. I began to realize that I had been lying to myself all along.

Then, one day, I was recommended to read a book by Napoleon Hill, "Think and Grow Rich," which profoundly shifted my thinking. It fueled my desire to learn more and explore the area of personal development and the power of the mind. I was seeking knowledge and reading all the time. The more I dove into the self-help world, the more I connected to my authentic self and understanding of who I truly am. I started reflecting more often on my thoughts and emotions and challenging my beliefs by digging deeper into their origin.

As a result, I allowed myself to feel whenever an emotion would come up or be triggered by interactions. I would address each emotion by sitting with it, naming it, feeling it, and letting it go. The more I thought about it, the less power it had over me later. Sometimes, I would journal as I went through those emotions to describe how and why I felt. It also helped me see them for what they were and create space between my true self and those temporary emotions. Eventually, I started feeling much lighter and happier than ever since I was no longer avoiding and resisting but welcoming any emotion that might show up. It was indeed a path to freedom and peace when I finally decided to face what I had been scared of for so long.

Moreover, the connection between my behavior and how I used to think became evident. I decided to invest in my personal development to see what's possible and what my life is all about. Eventually, I hired a mindset coach to help me heal, let go of all the conditioning, and grow into the best version of myself. It was the best decision ever since I finally released so many hidden self-limiting beliefs that would sabotage my success and prevent me from making the right choices in life. It felt like a heavy weight had been lifted from my chest, and now I could breathe again.

Therefore, I regained my power by becoming honest with myself and responsible for everything I experienced daily. Over time, I realized that I used to have a victim mindset since I always blamed people, circumstances, and events for the way I was feeling or for lacking something in life.

Understanding that I was the one choosing my thoughts that evoked certain feelings and led to particular actions, which consequently brought me the outcome I experienced. Seeing cause and effect law in motion for myself as I became mindful and present here and now gave me a new outlook on life. I was no longer procrastinating, making excuses, and feeling not enough, but rather, I was taking imperfect actions consistently, which, in turn, built my self-confidence by showing myself what I could accomplish. I developed a strong belief in myself, my skills and abilities, my expertise, and my core values. I loved who I was becoming since I started feeling like my true self and enjoying the process simultaneously.

Moreover, I saw many opportunities to express myself and apply my skills to serve others. The new life perspective became possible after practicing meditation and gratitude for some time and working with a coach. I would meditate at least once a day, almost every day, for 30 minutes or more. Every morning, I would set an intention for the day and list everything I was grateful for in my life. In turn, I deliberately focused more on the positive aspects of my life or what was going well for me. Gradually, I was enjoying my life experiences and feeling at peace. In my mind, I became free and detached from everyone and everything, but instead, I saw it all for what it was without labeling. I was no longer triggered when interacting with others since I constantly worked on processing and releasing my emotions. I felt a sense of freedom navigating through life experiences without any need to prove myself or to please others. I became non-reactive but at peace and calm since I knew my self-worth, which was enough. I realized I was responsible for my feelings and everything I had, so I gave myself everything I desired because I deserved it all.

Therefore, I prioritized my mental and physical health enough to make changes in my schedule on purpose. I knew I had to make changes by doing something different, so I reduced my hours working as a pharmacist and started studying for holistic health coaching certification in my free time. Then, I built my own coaching practice, Revive You, on the side. I have also co-founded a nutritional supplement company, Biomental, and started my own podcast, In Turn, to inspire and motivate others so they could create their lives by design. After interviewing hundreds of people and sharing their success stories, I developed the skill of active listening and connecting deeply in conversations. In addition, as I was coaching my clients, I clearly understood what was blocking them from getting the desired results. All that resulted from aligning with my true self and allowing myself to change and explore. I became highly productive, focused, creative, energized, and optimistic about my life. I started to bring that light and inspiration into interactions with others to uplift them in some way. I realized that my life purpose is bigger than myself, and my life has a significant meaning. I knew I was on the right path based on how good I felt in my body and mind.

Nothing is more liberating than knowing that I create my life the way I choose. No one can control your actions or hurt your feelings unless you let them. Nothing can trigger your emotions or set you off unless you let it. You can choose what you want to see in your life and who you want to become. You are in control of managing time daily to build your dream life and meaningful relationships with others. And it's true for each one of us. Be honest with yourself and ask: Do I exercise my power intentionally? How do I choose to spend my time daily? Am I creating my life by design? Can I look in the mirror and truly love the person who reflects back to me unconditionally?

Life always happens for your own benefit when you are presented with different experiences to learn and grow, even if you don't see it at that moment. Change constantly feels uncomfortable, but it is usually because it's unknown. By embracing change and uncertainty, you become more comfortable whenever you try something new. You build your inner strength and resilience when you choose not to give up on your dreams and keep moving forward. Honestly, it's getting easier each time you do it, and one day, you would look back and see that it was all worth it.

I am passionate about helping others become their best versions. That's why I focus on providing value such as services, products, tools, and practices through my work as a coach, a speaker, and an entrepreneur. If we let ourselves heal and grow, we will build healthier relationships with ourselves and others and have a better quality of life since we all deserve it. We can rewrite our stories at any time if we only decide. We were born to succeed and experience joy, love, and happiness. We are worthy by just being here without needing to prove it in any way whatsoever. It's time to reclaim your power.

 **ANNA BROOK** empowers others to live life in the full pursuit of their dreams. She is passionate about personal development and the power of the mind, so she started the *In Turn* podcast in 2022 to inspire and motivate her listeners. A believer in living life on her terms, Anna has worked as a pharmacist since 2016. During this time, she developed leadership and communication skills, as well as active listening and compassion towards her patients.

In addition to her career as a pharmacist, Anna is a certified holistic health coach and the co-founder of Biomental ®, a nutritional supplement company based in New York City. Always staying solutions-oriented, creative, and thinking outside of the box, Anna is determined to grow a culture of healthy, focused, and strong human beings by providing tools and support through her work. She loves to engage in deep conversations on the topics of self-help and mental health. In her spare time, she enjoys reading books, cooking, meditating, and dancing tango.

Connect with Anna Brook
https://reviveyou.me
https://www.instagram.com/abrook1111

What do you do when you think you have it all figured out, and your world collapses? Kim is telling in her story the nightmare she went through. She ended up in a deep abyss, almost lost in the labyrinth of demons, when one unexpected phone call through her the lifebuoy. No matter how deep we fall, there is always a way out. However, it is up to each one of us to grab the lifebuoy and say yes.

— *Sabine Kvenberg*

BREAKING THE CHAINS

by Kim Groshek

Power resonates when we are connected with our hearts and grounded in instinct. As Spiritual beings, we are pure love, and our soul guides us to create exactly what we need to experience and design for our lives.

I HAD ALWAYS been ambitious and driven, riding the wave of the computer science trend. I was on top of the world; everything seemed to go as planned. I worked full-time, was at the peak of my career, and finally obtained the director role I had always aspired to.

Then, one fateful morning, as I sat working at my desk early, the CEO, my direct superior, walked into my office and said the words that would shake my world: "Pack up your bags. You're fired. Get out of here."

I was blindsided, stunned, and confused. I didn't receive an explanation or any indication of what I had done wrong – kicked out and let go. What did I do wrong? I never got an explanation as to why. It felt like a sudden free fall into a deep black hole. I packed up my belongings. I tried to keep tears from spilling. My legs were heavy as I walked to my car. I threw my items in the back, sat in the driver's seat, turned the ignition, and drove home.

What happened? I had always wanted to move up in my career, especially being an employee for a company in the chains of rules, boundaries, and glass ceilings. Every time I tried, I'd hit a glass ceiling, be taken advantage of, or be not appreciated. Everything I had worked for my entire life taught me to get there on time, do the right thing, work hard to figure things out and do my best.

The day after, it all came crashing down; I got out of bed but then went to the couch and lay down, wrapped in an afghan all day. I slept, and that one day of inaction turned into months.

This person starkly contrasts the person I had always been – someone who worked diligently, aimed for perfection, and persevered through challenges. I had earned my degrees, pursued my career, and juggled motherhood alongside it all. I even took on part-time teaching at the university while managing a full-time job and caring for my daughter.

I spent six months stuck in the abyss. I barely recognized myself. I couldn't muster the strength to get up. I told myself stories about my worthlessness, sabotaging myself, and telling myself stories about how I'm not good enough. I didn't understand why it happened and decided then that I could no longer rely on anyone. I had tumbled into a pit of despair and depression. It wasn't just about sadness but a deep sense of hopelessness. I had nightmares and wasn't able to get myself out. I realize that my fear has always trapped me. The shadow gets the light, and until I'm at peace with myself, there will not be peace with the world.

For several months, my family and friends tried to cheer me up. A window of opportunity opened when I got a call from someone who believed in me despite my mess. She insisted that I could significantly improve an organization dealing with compliance problems.

I initially said, "No." However, she was persistent and kept calling and nagging me. I couldn't get past how hurt and humiliated I was. I was in the depths of my despair. I eventually dragged myself and accepted the offer. Getting out there felt good. I ended up getting back on my feet. It took some time, and I started feeling better about myself after a few months. I had to trust that it would all work out okay; it was pretty scary then.

I decided to take a step forward. I incorporated regular movement and exercise into my routine, knowing that it would help release some of the tension and anxiety. I got a coach and became part of a supportive group. With the support I received and the newfound awareness of my fears, I started to relax. I realized that my fear wasn't a puzzle to be solved but a feeling to be worked through. This story was far from over, but I was determined to confront my fears and move forward with my business.

Sometimes, all it takes is the courage to pause, breathe, and face the monsters lurking in our minds. I had taken the first step on my journey towards overcoming my fear and finding success in my life and career.

I always had this scary dream. The monster in my dream, the one that haunted me for years, was a presence that I couldn't quite understand or articulate. I would walk into this dream, finding myself in an old house with three stories. The setting felt real, almost like a place from my distant past. The rooms were filled with various pieces of old furniture, creating a sense of nostalgia and eeriness.

But the most unsettling part of the dream was a massive, foreboding wall that stood before me. It had an oppressive aura, and I could feel a presence lurking behind it. This presence felt dangerous and menacing, though I couldn't see the actual form of the monster. It was as if I could sense its malevolence without being able to confront it directly.

Every night, I'd have this dream, and sometimes the monster would manifest in various ways, but I never saw it. It was an unshakable fear, a recurring nightmare that left me deeply disturbed.

The dream faded as time passed, and I moved on, but the memory of that menacing presence lingered. It reflected my inner fears and anxieties during my life's journey. The monster represented the unknown and the unspoken fears that had a grip on my subconscious.

In the group discussion, my coach suggested that I confront my fear, this metaphorical monster that had haunted me for so long. This prompted me to reflect on my experiences and the fears that had held me back. Through this process, I began to explore the depths of my subconscious, trying to understand the root causes of my anxieties and the fears that had limited my progress.

My nightmares filled with monsters were a powerful metaphor for the obstacles I had faced in life. It was an invitation to delve into the darkest corners of my mind and confront the shadows that had held me back for so long. The journey was challenging, but it was a necessary step in my quest to overcome my fears and move forward with my life.

We can emerge from the darkness. The combination of external and inner voices and my inner strength led me back. It's about listening to the whispers of opportunity and finding our way back to the light, even in the darkest times.

I got back on my feet again. Life has a way of presenting us with many valuable lessons. While on a retreat in Colorado, during my early morning walks in the mountains, I listened to the wind speaking through the pine trees while I walked straight into the big dark sky. This whole experience made me not fear the darkness, the patterns that plagued me in the past. I was strong enough.

I'm more available and reach out to my friends. I take time to pause and send funny voice messages to my friends, allowing them to witness my fun "nerd party." They appreciate it. It's not just about seeking their support; it's also about sharing laughter and shifting their perspectives. It's a two-way gift.

I've embraced sitting in silence. Whether in nature or the comfort of my home, being still in the quiet of my mind has become a powerful part of my pause practice. It's in those moments of silence that I find clarity and peace.

Ten years have passed since I experienced this dark time in my life. Today, I have my own business, working as a consultant. I am no longer employed by someone else or chained to a company.

At first, I didn't understand why I had to go through such an unsettling time in my life, but looking back, it is obvious. You can only connect the dots looking back. I had to overcome my fears and demons to emerge as my next best self. I would never have gained my power without going through that experience.

Getting fired freed me to enter the most creative years of my life. I changed. I felt free and confident outside the company's confines. I realized my full potential after this career shift.

Being a consultant and working with large companies gave me the confidence that I have what it takes, and people saw my value. CEOs of large corporations trusted me with more extensive assignments due to my skills and persistence. It was liberating and allowed me to grow and perform in ways I never felt possible in a business environment.

I remember an unexpected phone call from someone seeking an expert to address a critical issue in a global program position at a Fortune-100 conglomerate as they faced impending major fines. After persistent discussions, I ultimately accepted the contract.

I outlined my strategy for turning the struggling company around in a boardroom filled with skepticism. Staring at the senior executive, I emphasized, "Change isn't about quick fixes; it's about focusing on the genuine 'want' and 'intent' for lasting impact. Clients need to cut through the noise and add real value, not just chase fleeting solutions."

As I navigated through the complexities, I remembered the valuable lesson my grandmother taught me with a simple butterfly. The company's metamorphosis mirrored the transformation from a caterpillar to a butterfly—slow, deliberate, and focused on proper growth.

I had a flashback of what my grandma said about the extraordinary, beautiful process of becoming a butterfly. Grandma loved butterflies. Her living room had this beautiful picture of a monarch butterfly resting on a flower. You couldn't go into any of her rooms without seeing an image of a butterfly. After six months of my "incubation," I visited Grandma. Noticing all the butterfly trinkets in her home, I asked her, "Why do you like butterflies so much?" She said, "Because it is amazing how an ugly caterpillar can go inside a cocoon and emerge a beautiful butterfly, one Butterfly wing extracting at a time. Knowing what I went through, she said, "You didn't fail — you just haven't mastered it yet. You can," she said, "I believe you can." Then she gave me a big grandma hug. She had such a big heart.

Power resonates when we are connected with our hearts and grounded in instinct. As Spiritual beings, we are pure love, and our soul guides us to create exactly what we need to experience and design for our lives.

This is why I am thankful for my depression...

For 6 months, I suffered in complete darkness and pain without money, employment, or much hope. I was disabled emotionally, and I thought the quality of my life would not improve. I was forgotten by most of who I was and where I came from. For all this time, my voice was no longer relevant because I was labeled from the outside, but no one knew me on the inside. So why would I be thankful for such a nightmare? Because what didn't end my existence gave me unimaginable mental strength and an experience I will use to help millions. Instead of becoming a victim, I chose to become a warrior. What many don't realize is we all have a choice. When life gets filled with suffering, we can find ways to numb or even end the pain. Or we can choose to lean in, find the silver lining, and transform into something much greater. If you are ready to change your life, there is only one rule… NEVER EVER GIVE UP! Because life does get better.

Today, I know the spiritual reality of who I am. The power we possess is connection; love is connection vs. conflict and fear. This true power can positively affect millions. Many of us suppress our power by conflicting with ourselves because we fear how it will affect others and what responses we will get or are scared to make mistakes.

Since everything is personal, I do my best and love what I do. Do what makes me feel good and trust my gut. My heart and intuition somehow already know who I am. Not much else matters.

You already know that this power, your "Power," and your purpose can bring love into your life, your world, and the world as a whole. Like throwing a pebble in the water, water rings ripple. Love rooted in intuition is the pebble causing ripples that profoundly impact our lives.

Adopting our real potential is our superpower. Be brave and listen to your heart. I did it, and so can you. I went through the metamorphosis, just like the butterfly. The time of not moving, not knowing what I was about to become, was challenging but worth it. I found my wings, and let me tell you, it feels great up here.

KIM GROSHEK, CEO of Pause Power International and founder of the Spring Soiree Scholarship Foundation, holds an M.S., MBA, E-RYT® 500, and numerous certifications. As an international best-selling author, Groshek is the sole female business coach appointed ambassador at Large for women's advancement in Africa. Through her company, Pause Power Inc., and innovative coaching, clients have saved over $20 million by simplifying operations and embracing downtime. Kim, the "Pause Lady," advocates for success through strategic pauses and mental health coaching. She attains personal freedom by working remotely, fundraising for education and women-centric causes, and guiding others in financial discipline and emotional regulation. When she's not empowering others, you'll find her telling stories on stage, walking outside, swimming in the pool or cherishing moments with her family. Join Kim to create the life you deeply desire, both personally and in your business, to create a space where your confidence transitions into the life you've always envisioned.

Connect with Kim Groshek
https://kimgroshek.com
https://www.facebook.com/groups/pausesummitlive

Darlene was a guest on my show and shared her and her husband's amazing health recovery. Traumatic experiences and not taking care of yourself can lead to serious health challenges. How can you contain or reverse a condition by avoiding medication if this happens? In Darlene's story, you will learn that if life gives you adversities, in the end, it is for the greater good.
— *Sabine Kvenberg*

PAIN, PERSISTENCE, AND PURPOSE

by Darlene Greene

In the end, I've learned that physical pain pales in comparison to emotional pain but that any kind of pain can be more than just weathered and endured. When we embrace our pain, work through it, and learn from it, we can become a beacon of light for others.

IT IS NOT equitably distributed or experienced. Having the experience of pain opens our eyes to a world we never noticed. It opens our hearts to sense pain in others in a way we couldn't before.

If you had asked me in my youth to define pain, I would have only thought to describe a broken bone or something physical because I had experienced a fortunate upbringing. Perhaps I made up for that idyllic childhood as an adult, though. I've had friends tell me weekly that the challenges I faced with ex-husband number two (more on that later) should be a TLC movie. As an adult, I learned that the pain of physical injuries pales in comparison to emotional traumas that shatter our naivete and innocence.

I was a horrible judge of character and made terrible choices in my first two husbands. My sister and I sometimes jokingly blame our father, a man of such extraordinary character, honor, honesty, generosity, cheer, and love that it never occurred to us that all men weren't like that.

The disillusionment of my first marriage came like a lightning-fast sucker punch, only that lightning struck repeatedly. We had married the weekend I graduated and was commissioned an Ensign in the Navy. We stayed married for six years, but I knew in year one I had made a terrible mistake.

When emotional abuse turned to physical abuse, I knew I had to get out, or I might not survive it. As I was getting my affairs in order to separate, I discovered my husband had secretly spent all of our savings and had opened up a credit card I knew nothing about, racking up a great deal of debt. I have no idea where that money went or what he spent it on. As we worked through the property division, I took all the debt and left him with all the furniture, dishes, art, and the Porsche so he would think he was getting a great deal and maybe let me get away alive.

I shared the inner secrets of the abuse with only one girlfriend who lived nearby. She was incredibly dear to me. We took step aerobics class at the Pentagon together daily, talked on the phone endlessly, and went out weekly to find the best French onion soup in the Arlington, Alexandria, Washington DC area.

As hard as it was to go through a divorce and fear for my life in doing so, it paled in comparison to the gut-wrenching news that my ex-husband gleefully relayed that he and my girlfriend had been seeing each other for some time and were now taking trips out of town. My girlfriend had seen the blood, the wounds, even the scars that served as a memory of the violence I endured. She had listened to me pour my heart out. The fact that somewhere along the way, she had begun dating and sleeping with my ex and that she had not been the one to tell me was a betrayal that hurt for decades.

I thought I was being so much smarter and more careful before entering my second marriage, but Narcissists can be so shockingly charming. They can have credentials and successes that belie the evil in their soul and true inner being. Often, it is only after quite some time that we begin to catch a glimpse of their pretend persona. With husband number two the shock of it all came slowly, like a poisonous fog, suffocating me until I realized it truly would kill me from the inside out if I did not escape it. Narcissists are such believable liars, and I allowed my prefrontal cortex and reasoning to talk myself right out of the red flags I saw. I ignored the hairs that stood up on the back of my neck.

The marriage to my second husband also lasted six years. Still, in this one, I tried endless counseling, read hundreds of relationship books, and tried everything possible to keep it together because we had two amazing, beautiful daughters. However, nothing worked, and finally, I asked for a divorce because that was the best option for all of us. I worked hard to keep my young daughters completely unaware, sometimes writing court declarations all night while they slept and pretending all was fine while awake.

The girls and I all had regular therapy. Still, my body caved under the pressures of working as a US Navy Commander, single parenting, fighting in court, worrying endlessly every time I had to hand the girls over to him for his visitations, and trying to make ends meet, all while pretending everything was fine in front of the girls. I suppose it's not surprising I was diagnosed with Post Traumatic Syndrome (PTSD), Chronic Fatigue Syndrome, Fibromyalgia, Hypothyroidism, Migraines, and Postural Orthostatic Tachycardia (POTs) over the years.

Relief came when I had military orders to my next duty station as the Commanding Officer of the Navy Operational Support Center, Phoenix, AZ. It was a blessing. It allowed me to get distance between my ex and me. The car was loaded with our clothing only because, again, I left marriage two without so much as a soup spoon, and we were headed to Arizona.

In that final Navy tour, I led a team of amazing patriots, including a staff of 1200 Navy and Marine reservists. It was a rewarding time during my career.

Although I had sworn I would never date again, much less ever marry again, through the most serendipitous of events, the angels delivered a solid gold man of incredible character, honesty, integrity, unparalleled patience, and a tremendous sense of humor. Jim, a Navy Captain and Naval Aviator brought sunshine, peace, and joy into our lives in a way I had not thought possible. Jim and I started seeing each other by doing "group things" because I was NOT dating. Eventually, we dropped the chaperone. After years of dating, the girls pleaded for me to marry Jim. We married in 2007 and recently celebrated our 16th wedding anniversary. Our marriage has been delightful, easy, fun, warm, loving, and a true partnership among best friends. Our girls have been blessed to see what a great marriage looks like, and I gained two wonderful adult sons in the deal. We were living a fairy tale life until the unthinkable occurred.

The clues moved in with a subtlety that defied their gravity. Was Jim drinking more than I knew? Why was he completely blacking out on conversations and events of the night before? When he couldn't remember which remote to use to watch our favorite nightly TV show, I asked, "Do you feel like you are having challenges with your memory?" "Yes," Jim said.

Jim was diagnosed with Early Alzheimer's. Early Alzheimer's is more aggressive, sometimes having a lifespan of 5-10 years. I started reading and researching. The "best" drug on the market that was recently released caused brain bleeds in 50% of people with Jim's APOE 4/4 gene type. Stem cells seemed to be the most promising treatment. We went to Mexico to get IV stem cells and stem cell injections at great expense, approximately $10,000 a time for each of us, and we both got them quarterly for a year. As I added up our medical expenses that year, they topped $140,000, and I prayed for a miracle and a way to not go bankrupt as we tried to keep Jim present and alive. We saw no improvement from the stem cells, and the decline continued.

We tried many other treatments like hyperbaric chamber and ozone therapy. We eliminated mold toxins and removed sugar, white and wheat flour, and all bad oils from our diet. We began eating only non-genetically modified (non-GMO) foods and trying to keep everything organic. We added loads of vegetables every day. We cycled in and out of ketosis to get ketones to his brain. I jokingly told Jim, "If it tastes good, spit it out!" and we would laugh. Jim was a darn good sport about it all. We began to exercise six times a week.

Still, the decline continued. Jim slept 3.5 hours a day and fell asleep at 7 pm. He was disengaged from conversations. They were just too challenging for him. When he did engage, he was three conversations behind. He asked the same questions seven times in three minutes, challenging every fiber of my being to remain patient and act like it was the first time I had heard the question.

But what broke my heart was that he was no longer trying to be funny, which is core to his personality. At this point, Jim was truly just a shell of his former self. I had lost him and quietly grieved the loss of my super-savvy, smart, and funny best friend.

To make matters worse, I missed the last three stairs in our house and landed so hard on my left foot that I broke my foot and snapped one ankle ligament entirely and another one 90%. Some of my best care provider coping mechanisms (exercise, pickleball, walks around the neighborhood) came to an abrupt halt, and I was in severe pain for months. I discovered asking Jim to get me an ice water was too much for him and my frustration, disappointment, and grief pushed me right into a full-blown depression. I wanted to cry every day.

A friend who knew I had tried stem cells recommended LifeWave's photo biomodulation patches and said it had completely changed her family's life. I learned that this small quarter-sized patch helps elevate a very powerful peptide in our bodies, copper peptide GHK-Cu. Following the same process that occurs when we are out in the sun and our bodies make vitamin D or melanin, the patch uses the process of photo biomodulation to activate and elevate our GHK-Cu levels. I was excited and skeptical when I learned that one of the many benefits of elevating GHK-Cu is activating our dormant stem cells. I had not known that when we are 30 years old, half of our stem cells are dormant, and nearly all are dormant when we are 60.

The first week of patching, we both experienced miracles. First, Jim didn't nap at all! He didn't even fall asleep during our evening TV show. Moreover, it was like a dam had broken, and two years of conversation had come rushing out. He was so much chattier and more engaged in conversation. In those discussions, he was not speaking a word salad that made no sense, rather, he was "with it," replying quickly and appropriately. He didn't ask me the same questions repeatedly, either. (Thank you, dear Lord.)

My first day of patching was the first day in five months that I was relieved of pain. I couldn't believe it. That week, I had an extraordinary boost in energy, even waking before my alarm clock, which rarely happened. In the first couple of weeks, I noticed a very dramatic improvement in my depression. It lifted and dissipated and left in its wake a calm, less anxious, more patient, lighter, and joy-filled mood.

Over the next few months, I saw more and more improvement in Jim's overall health. He regained his sense of smell, which he had lost 15 years ago, and the ability to whistle. But what warmed my heart was that Jim was funny again! And flirty! He was back to his original personality! I had my Jim back!

While we have a long way to go, I feel like it's an amazing sign that he is regaining neuro skills, and he is certainly living a higher quality of life – which means I'm living a higher quality of life!

Over time, other things improved for me as well: My rosacea cleared (after being there for years and stubbornly defying dermatologists' efforts), and my weekly headaches just stopped. Not only did I no longer worry about making sure I was always carrying my migraine medicine, but I completely lost track of where any of it was. My body aches that had been a part of my Fibromyalgia went away as well.

After all the positive impact we both experienced, I could not help but share it with family and friends. I kept learning more and more about the capabilities of the patches. I found an entire community of like-minded, supportive, and generous people with a deep passion for helping others with their health.

The overcoming of pain turned into a new career for me, passionately helping to spread the word and seeing others get results. This new LifeWave family grows for me every day. The silver lining of Jim's Alzheimer's will always be that it has helped me help others as I developed friendships worldwide from Germany, England, India, Switzerland, South Africa, and across the US, which I would never have otherwise met.

In the end, I've learned that physical pain pales in comparison to emotional pain but that any kind of pain can be more than just weathered and endured. It can serve to remove a filter that covers our eyes and eradicate the obliviousness that accompanies our innocence and naivete. It can be used to connect to others to understand better, empathize, and help them. I don't know that anyone goes through a full life without pain. Do we allow ourselves to be transparent and vulnerable enough to share it with others, find the support we need, and leverage it for good? When we embrace our pain, work through it, and learn from it, we can become a beacon of light for others.

DARLENE GREENE has over 26 years of experience in executive leadership and senior management positions across diverse industries, including positions such as Vice President of Strategic Technology Partner at McAfee (Intel), Dean of Culver Girls Academy, Director of Client Services for HyeTech Networks and Security, and Senior Director LifeWave Stem Cell Activation Technology. During her 20 years of military experience, she earned her MBA and held three Commanding Officer positions, including serving as base commander overseeing 1200 personnel. Darlene created the Returning Warrior Weekend Workshop in 2006 to help military and their spouses reintegrate successfully, a program still in existence across the country today.

After experiencing the amazing results for herself, and watching family and friends have their own miracles, Darlene's passion is helping people elevate their GHK-CU peptide to activate their stem cells, repair their DNA, reverse age, and get out of pain through the latest photobiomodulation technology.

Connect with Darlene Greene
https://iamreverseaging.com
https://www.linkedin.com/in/darlenegreene

Victoria bought my book Unlock Your Full Potential. We lived in the same city, and she wanted to meet me to express her gratitude. Little did we know that this meeting evolved into a deep friendship. Victoria is a woman of strength, tenacity, and determination. She shares her journey from having the dream life to having nothing and how she overcame one of her darkest times to rise again..

— Sabine Kvenberg

THE FORCE THAT HOLDS US

by Victoria Ochoa

My life fell apart, but picking up the pieces, I learned there is healing in nature, strength in faith, security in education, and support in sisterhood.

SITTING AT AN impromptu desk by the fireplace, arranging donation pick-up, I slowly looked around the empty house, going room to room in my mind to make sure I did not miss any of the few remaining items that were not in storage.

The emptiness of the house started to dawn on me. I felt its sadness steadily creep up into my body, its fear grab tight to my heart, its disbelief tangle itself around my lungs. I CAN'T BREATHE! Where did my beautiful, perfect white picket fence life go?!

How did all the beautiful memories of laughter, daily conversations during family meals, celebrations, Halloween, Thanksgiving, Christmas, birthdays, grandparents' visits, family TV nights, snuggles on the couch with my husband — poof, just vanish?!

Where is my beautiful house that I decorated with so much love?

Many mornings, before everybody woke up, I would sit in the family room, holding my tea, looking around in delight, so proud and content with my life. I was there again, in disbelief, contemplating a very different scene. I CAN'T BREATHE!

My Daughter and I had just dropped off my soon-to-be X-husband at the airport, and then I drove her to her perfect private high school in a beautiful Atlanta neighborhood. My son was at his cozy little middle school down the road from our house in the Georgia suburbs with all his friends that he knew forever, clueless, waiting for the school day to be over so he could go to his friend's Birthday party.

My sister — who was thousands of miles away — was chatting on and off with me on the computer, thank GOD she was online! I CAN'T BREATHE! I texted her. "Calm down, everything is going to be OK." she texted back. She called me and calmed me down as she had always done, with her big sister's command.

She explained in her matter-of-fact doctor's voice that I was having a panic attack. She instructed me to calm down, open my heart, and breathe deeply. Slowly, my stunned heart stopped beating a thousand miles per hour, my breath relaxed, and I was left crying helplessly, releasing the scare. She told me not to worry that my sister-in-law was on her way to help me.

My sister-in-law came rushing to my rescue! She dragged me to the Mexican restaurant nearby, where they had rockstar Margaritas. I lost count at 3, I think I drank them all. I can only recall infinite sadness and loads of tears. I cried and cried and cried while my sister-in-law offered so much compassion. She was there listening to me, consoling me, being quiet, being present across the table, ordering more margaritas for me ...and then I was home, lying on a rug, the only accessory left in the family room.

There, I continued to weep miserably. She told me that she had never seen me cry so much. Then I fell asleep, I have no idea how I managed to let her know that my son was waiting at school.

My life was about to go into a rollercoaster, the most difficult part to bear was that it was also going to take my precious children on the same shitty ride. I still have yet to recover from the extreme guilt I feel that they had to come along.

The three of us were left like a deer in the headlights while my ex-husband took off to another country to start his new life with his mistress. She was 6 years younger than me and had just gotten a pair of new boobs. He had a lot to look forward to.

My ex-husband and I had our own company and worked with her employer. She collaborated on different projects. They had been collaborating in different ways for a while. IMAGINE THE ANGER!

After short selling the house, leaving all our precious belongings in storage, and packing our necessities and clothes, our life as we knew it was OVER.

Where does one pick up from there?

How does a mom find the grit to keep going when she is exhausted and heartbroken, and all her energy is focused on wanting revenge?! "She-Devil" had nothing on me. The outrage is too enormous to even fit in all the books written! You know what I mean if you have been in a similar situation!

We moved in with my sister-in-law, who gave us the guest room where we set up my daughter's daybed trundle and an ottoman. We placed all of our clothing and their school supplies in the closet and made the beds. Their eyes were about to pop out of their heads. My beautiful children were scared and seemed hopeless, the energy in the room was harsh. I WAS SO HEARTBROKEN!

The look on their faces broke my heart into a million pieces, but I managed to compose myself, and with certainty, I told them: "It will be ok, give me three months, and we will move on." I spent three months in purgatory, watching our cash flow dwindle while I was looking for a job.

I was a successful marketing executive and gave up my job to build our company. Who knew; It was 2010, and shit was about to hit the fan?! It was bad timing to invest in a new venture, such is life. I FELT SO HELPLESS.

Somehow, I knew that despite this all, I had the power to overcome it.

I tried to keep my children's lives as normal as possible. I took them to little dinner luxuries within our tight budget, I drove a great distance to take my daughter to school every day. I set up playdates for my son to see his buddies and not feel forgotten. He was such a trooper, making new friends in an inner-city middle school environment he knew nothing about. He always kept a happy attitude to cheer me up. We all made a huge effort. I was ¼ myself and had to be mom and dad.

Three months went by. We experienced so much in that short time that it seems to me like a year!

The biggest saving grace was being with Mother Nature. I learned that from my parents. Growing up, they took me and my siblings to experience and enjoy nature in all ways possible. When we lived in a big city in Colombia, it was imperative that on weekends, we visited the countryside, jumped in the creeks and rivers, visited farms, and discovered beautiful mountain scenery, which is still breathtaking there!

That beautiful gift I was brought up with came in handy when I was longing for my home within me. I found solitude in Kennesaw Mountain, a short walk right by my sister-in-law's house. Every day, after my children were at school, my nature temple would call me, "Come to me, sweet child, and calm yourself."

My mind was a ball of mixed-up confusion, with enormous amounts of anger and an immeasurable desire for dark, painful revenge. How was I going to become whole? Where could I untangle this ugliness that cluttered my thinking? I knew I was not this angry, hateful person, and I had to get rid of her quickly!

As I walked, I breathed deeply, like my sister taught me, to calm my mind. As I looked, I chose to see the beauty of the sun's rays peeking through the trees. As I listened, I heard the wind shaking the leaves. A precious healing symphony of nature was performed for me so I could heal. I filled my mind with LOVE. The amazing love of creation surrounded me in this beautiful place.

One hateful thought at a time, I started reversing the negative ideas in my head and replacing them with a vision that was loaded with love. The hardest part was that this love was directed at the very people who were, in my mind, guilty of my suffering. I had to be very aware and catch myself to make the switch.

I slowly started to understand, forgive, humanize the experience, and return to myself. MY THOUGHTS WERE NO LONGER ANYBODY ELSE'S BUT MINE.

This serene strength also helped me keep my grit and focus on finding a new beginning. That also means getting a steady paycheck to support myself and my children.

I am thankful for my education back in my young adult years.

We often hear that education is the one thing nobody can take away from us, and I can't agree more. I never gave up on it despite hating some of the classes I attended. The running joke at family dinners was my dad asking me what semester I was in. Holding my nervous laugh, I would pick up pieces of semesters and hop from one credit to another, babbling about my classes. In time, I learned that he was not in a rush as long as I got a degree, and that I did!

Two years after getting my Bachelor's, I enrolled in my Master's program. Well, the thing is, I was managing a company and also got pregnant with my daughter, which added a bit of a challenge for both of us. When she was born, I took her along to my study groups. I would nurse her under a little blanket while my peers and I were deep in discussion. Sometimes, when she wasn't fast asleep, she would peek out and join our study sessions.

So I was always ready to make my education count, even more, this time around, because I was starting over, and my two children and I depended on it!

It did pay off. Three months into my job search, I got a first confirmation call from my recruiter! The skies opened up, trumpets were sounding, and angels were singing, "Victoria, there is a company that wants to fly you in for an interview." Hallelujah Baby! After two companies, three flights, many interviews, countless hours on job boards, and months of sleeplessness, I got a new job.

Oh, and of course, heartfelt S.O.S. prayers, like a helpless bird holding her chicks in the nest during a storm. God, please get us out of this mess!

When I was still married in my white picket fence life, I used to visit a catholic church close by, Saint Michael ArchAngel, that had a beautiful chapel open for prayer all day. I would love to go and find solitude there.

I recall one day, a lady in her mid-30s walked up to the altar, dropped herself to her knees, and bent in a dramatic gesture of surrender. I could feel the pain! My eyes watered as my little problems became erased compared to whatever made her curl into insignificance, asking for help. I felt so sorry, all I could do was send this stranger my prayers.

I didn't know that a year later, I would be the one dropping to my knees.

Of course, I recognize the glory of God's loving hands in all this mess! Of course, I was praying hard. Of course, I knew we would be fine! When I told my children, "Give me three months", I knew that we had a higher power looking over us. As my mom would say: " Dios no ha muerto", God's not dead. God is alive! I will never forget that.

I will also never forget all my beautiful sisters who rescued us in many ways. What would we have done without them?

I remember my neighbor and I were walking our kids to the bus stop. When she asked me how I was doing, I broke down in tears. She was the first person I told about my divorce. We sat down under the huge dogwood tree in my front yard and had a long conversation. She gave me her shoulder to cry on.

Another unexpected angel showed up to help. A long-lost friend from my hometown in Colombia got her husband and a friend to drive a moving truck and help me put my belongings into storage. She gave me her family's Sunday.

Two years later, I returned to donate most of the things I had held on to, thinking someday I would be back to how it was. Life changes and does not wait for our memories to catch up, nor does it wait for belongings that no longer fit our new world. Letting go of the remainder of my past life was one of the hardest tests I have had to endure.

The support of my beautiful friend, whom I met through our daughter's basketball, gave me strength. She helped me and my daughter sort through memories, lift boxes, and take the smaller items to donation. She always gave me unconditional moral support and friendship with her warm smile.

This unexpected life also gave me new sisters, like my intense friend from Sarasota, who matched my intensity. She plugged me into a new world, introduced me to her friends, and invited us on boat rides with her handsome husband. She also taught me that "men are dessert". Maybe someday, when I truly master it, I will share her wisdom.

From the beginning, my sister-in-law was always there supporting us. She took us under her wing to weather the storm and start to heal. She shared her beautiful home, her privacy, her peace. What would we have done without her safe haven?

With courage, calm intensity, and maturity, my daughter became my sister through all this. She was our mother hen and my best friend. Always holding me accountable when I started to lose track. She still does.

And, of course, MY AMAZING BIG SISTER, who, since I can remember, has always been there to come to my aid. She taught me how to breathe despite the world falling into pieces around me! I miss her dearly. I wish I could have taught her how to breathe again. Maybe there is a calming breath in heaven, sis.

There were brothers, too. But that is another story.

Sometimes, I jokingly say that if there is a past life, I must have run over a nun. Why did I have to endure this?! In all seriousness, I have also accepted all these experiences as lessons I have learned from. Maybe someone else will, too. My life fell apart, but picking up the pieces, I learned there is healing in nature, strength in faith, security in education, and support in sisterhood.

Most of all, I learned that my biggest driving force and power came from my children. Knowing they depended on me and that if I dropped and stayed there, they would too. So I came up again and again and always will for them. They gave me their courage.

In the end, the power is always within me. It is this all-encompassing love force that holds our amazing universe together. May this force be with you, too.

VICTORIA OCHOA, a seasoned marketing professional with over 25 years in Fortune 100 corporate leadership, holds a Master's in Marketing and a Bachelor's in Business from esteemed Colombian institutions. Her expertise lies in driving impactful marketing strategies.

Transitioning from corporate roles, Victoria now channels her entrepreneurial spirit and passion for well-being towards contributing to a better world. Dedicated to promoting sustainable lifestyles and prioritizing well-being and joy, she extends her extensive marketing knowledge to wellness companies, practitioners, and well-being enthusiasts.

Victoria's academic accomplishments include a specialized Master's degree in Marketing from EAFIT in Colombia. Complementing her professional journey, she is a certified Kundalini Yoga Instructor, Well-being Coach, and PPR Pickleball Coach.

Based in sunny Florida, Victoria actively engages in promoting alternative health, the outdoors, and vibrant communities. As a proud mother of two healthy young adults, she embodies the values of well-being and fulfillment she champions professionally.

Connect with Victoria Ochoa
https://www.linkedin.com/in/mavicochoa
thewellbeinglife@gmail.com

The perspective Birgitta gives us is a beautiful insight into who we can become. Her deep sense of being authentically herself comes through with each interaction. Her travels and experiences, from abuse and trauma to breaking free, are the focal point of the story in this chapter. You will find lots of wisdom in her words. I hope it will spark something within you to reflect upon.

— *Sabine Kvenberg*

A JOURNEY TO THE LIGHT WITHIN

by Birgitta Visser

I wouldn't be who I am today or walking the path I am on now, so I am grateful for all my experiences. Pain is a blessing in disguise; it brings us back to the wonderment of the very breath of our soul.

AS I SIT here on my terrace, lost in my thoughts, in the warmth of the late Costa Blanca autumn sun, watching the palm leaves sway gently in the breeze over the terracotta rooftops, the occasional parrot noisily flying by and the sea quietly beckoning in the distance, I reminisce about my life and all the marvelous yet often beautifully disastrous experiences I created and challenged myself with. To sit here in the absolute stillness of myself is a far cry from who I once was, am now, and "ultimately am still becoming." Life hasn't been easy, but I wouldn't have it any other way; without these valuable experiences, I would not be who I am today, and I treasure that above all else.

2023 has been a year of reflection, healing, and constant transformation. I have worked for an oil and gas corporation for too many hours, with barely a weekend off. In addition, doing all my spiritual work, promoting my current book, and working on my next book, I was burning the candle at both ends. I suffered a burnout nearly twice and knew I needed a change.

I decided to relocate from the UK to Spain. With the rest going to charity, I sold most of what I had and hopped on a plane to Orihuela Costa with a couple of suitcases. When I got the keys to the rental, I was greeted by immense grease and dust, with more than half the stuff left by the previous elderly owners. Regardless of how exhausted I was, I managed to clean the place from top to bottom, with several issues, including a tap going haywire, breaking off after turning it, drenching me completely, and finally settling in.

While I agree that the grass is not always greener, there is a significant difference between avoiding our problems versus purposefully moving forward. Our choices shape our reality; we have the power to consciously create change, make enlightened decisions, and welcome life's journey with open arms.

Before being born in 1974, in the old town of Spijkenisse in the Netherlands, an old fishing and farming village along the Oude Maas River, I, like you, sat down with the council and my chosen guides, ticking all the boxes of possible traumatic lessons for my soul to evolve in this school of life. We may have thought it would be a walk in the park. Still, once we popped out of the womb as the once innocent baby, we forgot why we came here in the first place, getting lost in this earthly jungle, this *'Terra-rium,'* being conditioned according to the created societal norms of how we should live our lives, rather than living our lives according to the status quo and song of our soul.

The first traumatic experience I remember came at the tender age of ten when I was abused by a friend of the family in Kuala Lumpur. The next one hit even harder. I lost my dad to coronary heart disease at the age of fourteen, after having returned to Holland, with my mum having to take care of two teenagers and a debt to start with. It was the first time I experienced a throbbing headache. I was hoping that the next day, when I woke up, it would all have been a bad dream, and my dad would come walking through that door, but unfortunately, it remained a harsh reality that we all had to deal with.

Moving back to the Netherlands from Malaysia was a culture shock. Being tall and skinny and having no self-esteem, I was bullied at school while also being terrified of boys. At fifteen, I started working part-time at a department store, my sister at sixteen, and we would pay rent to our mum to help her with the monthly bills. She taught us to have responsibility for our own lives in many areas and to have respect for others.

I walked around like the Hunchback of Notre Dame, not wanting to be seen as I hated myself and the way I looked. My mum put me in a modeling course to help correct my posture, seeing I carried the weight of the world on my shoulders, but it didn't help; I remained as rigid within myself as ever, unable to let go of my deep-seated traumatic experiences. At the age of nineteen, after watching an episode of the Oprah Winfrey show discussing abuse, I finally told my mum that I had suffered at the hands of a family friend. Even so, it took many years and much healing to come from hating myself to loving myself more wholesomely.

Many make modeling out to be this glitzy world of glamour; however, behind the façade lies a superficial industry that can be degrading. Going to castings, I felt like a cow being branded in a cattle market, either being given a yay or nay. You constantly get judged on your outer appearance, and being rejected repeatedly dented my self-confidence. I would often retreat to my room in tears, struggling to understand what was wrong with me and why agencies dismissed me as if I were a nobody. Beauty is merely skin deep; our physical appearance does not determine nor define who we are; our inner qualities do. I have been sexually harassed and assaulted and also had photographers and stylists who, when adjusting my clothes, would feel my body up far more than necessary, with me tucking the experiences away in the very archives of my mind like I always did.

This world was not for me, yet these dualities of experiences served to me on my platter along the buffet of life were meant to help me sweat the chilies, giving me a better understanding of life and myself.

The year 2000 hit me hard; my stepdad passed away from cancer. My mum leaned on me, and I leaned on my so-called "friends" for support. But they brushed aside my grief, only wanting to see my happy face. So, I turned to a different comfort that would make me forget. Popping pills became my pastime. Ecstasy, coke, molly, you name it. I'd taken too many one night that I blacked out, waking up the next day with zero memory of what went down. That was my wake-up call. I went cold turkey, quitting everything at once. I rolled into several extremely dysfunctional relationships, suffering from vaginismus well into my forties, a condition where unhealed emotional trauma stored deep in the body's memory causes the vaginal muscles to involuntarily tighten up making intimacy difficult. On top of that, I was about as swift at learning life's lessons as a turtle on sedatives. I suffered from daily throbbing headaches but always soldiered on, never bowing down to defeat, having regimented coping mechanisms in place, working like a maniac, and starving myself, which only became more prominent as I got older.

I was in an abusive relationship and needed to get out fast. In just two days, my mother helped me move from Holland to the UK where I rented a place near her. My ex was a crack addict, unable to overcome his inner demons. He became involved with the Dutch Crips gang, who have long profited from illegal activities like gambling, drug dealing, pimping, theft, and robbery in LA. Desperate for his next fix, he stole from them and was held for ransom. I aided the police, who rescued him and deported him back to the US. The Dutch Crips' leader threatened to kill me if he ever found me. I spiraled to an all-time low, overwhelmed with emptiness and sadness that I couldn't shake. I was probably borderline depressed and downed a whole box of Ibuprofen, which only gave me a good night's sleep and eased my splitting headache. It was a weak attempt on my own life, and I knew then that I needed help. I had to put on my big girl pants and find a way forward rather than allow myself to be continuously pulverized by my experiences. I opted to walk the holistic route by finding a Reiki healer, my saving grace, studying under her and attaining levels 1 & 2.

When we become 'ill,' we become imbalanced of love and light; we are at a "dis-ease" with ourselves, rather than in sync, all because we are trying to confine ourselves into being someone we are not. The energy flowing through our meridian system becomes blocked because of our unhealed experiences, causing our physical essence to suffer as we have clogged the pot. We often hoard all these unhealed experiences in the archives of our minds, causing these to eventually burst at the seams.

Rather than subscribing to more issues, I started to unsubscribe and clear the pile of junk of my experiences. I realized that my energetic distortion was a created concept of myself into this chosen reality – for what I ingested into my subconscious mind is what manifested into my physical reality. Recognizing and becoming conscious of my patterns was the key to my inner well-being and healing.

I studied many other healing modalities, including Angelic Reiki, Holistic Nutrition, Addiction studies, Quantum Touch, EFT, and Meditation, absorbing it all like a SpongeBob and eventually teaching some modalities.

In 2016, I had another epiphany, going through yet another very dysfunctional relationship. This person would not relent, holding on for dear life, having an immense fear of losing me while going through his own trauma. Even though the relationship was highly toxic for both of us, we turned out the better for it. I see him as having been a wonderful teacher to my then very wayward soul, and both he and my other ex have healed their inner demons and turned their lives around for the better. At the time, however, I was close to the end of my wits, in a constant fight or flight mode, hating the very essence of him. I also hated the very essence of myself, and thus, he was a mere reflection of everything that I had chosen to be but was not.

I often cried myself to sleep on the floor, and exasperated; I asked the Universe and my guides for help. And help they did, for even in my haze, I finally became aware of the signs following the breadcrumb trail in the form of thoughts and people dotted across my path. Taking my sister's advice, who completely turned her own life around by overcoming her trauma, I did a Kambo frog cleanse, an intense shamanic purging ceremony, cleansing and healing the mind, body, and soul. It is not for the faint of heart as it is highly physical, yet to me, it was a compelling way of moving the hardened energy within me, kicking my ego out of the driver's seat, and listening to the voice of my soul. Two weeks later, after spirit nudged me out the door, I went to a fair, where I met my former mentor, an Akashic record healer, who helped me walk through my past lives to disentangle the energetic ties between me and my Floridian ex. We don't often realize that we sometimes get caught up in the cycle of karma.

I learned to channel after attending a workshop, eventually learning Light Language several years later. Don't think that you cannot channel because you can! Merely sit down with a notepad and pen, take a few deep breaths, and say to your Guides and the Universe, "I AM ready to receive." Don't think; just allow whatever comes, to flow through you naturally. It doesn't matter if it's just a sentence; it's not a competition. If you have angel or ascended master cards, shuffle these, pick one, and repeat the same exercise.

I lost my childhood to trauma, having to find my way in this world by fixing the entangled, broken mess within myself, having constantly allowed fear and shame to condition me. I wouldn't be who I am today or walking the path I am on now, so I am grateful for all my experiences. Pain is a blessing in disguise; it brings us back to the wonderment of the very breath of our soul. No matter how lost we feel or how severe the abuse we experienced, no one can rescue you from the depths of despair and hopelessness but yourself.

Life is meant for us to follow our passions, doing what makes our heart sing and soul dance in alignment with the movement of the I AM powerhouse that we are. And I certainly don't work the weekends any longer, killing myself for a job that would replace me in the space of a week if I were to drop dead. Meditation is what helped me nip this in the butt. People often think it is a mere form of juju or a waste of time because that is what society has led us to believe. Yet, breathwork helps realign and refocus our thoughts in the here and now.

Any trauma we go through is like a proverbial boomerang that keeps coming back to us until we learn to listen, using the pain as a stepping stone to healing ourselves and hearing our inner voice again. Life may not always be easy; I, too, am still a work in progress, but there is nothing that cannot be overcome to become the best version of the *hue* that is you. Returning to our authentic nature means becoming more conscious and more aware in all we do; rather than having our minds full, we become mindful. I firmly believe that talking about trauma very openly helps us heal. I hope to have inspired you by telling my story, planting that thought-for-thought seed, assisting others in telling their own stories, and knowing they're not alone. As St. Germain always says, *"Life is merely a return to love, nothing more, nothing less."*

As I sit here on my terrace, with the sun sinking below the horizon, I find myself lost in contemplation. The fading light casts long shadows that echo the reflections in my mind. I savor this quiet moment to honor the journey that brought me here. Though the road has been long, each twist and turn has gifted me wisdom. While storms have battered me, in their wake, they gave me insights. As dusk approaches, I stand centered in the calm between adventures. The next sunrise will illuminate fresh opportunities and new lessons to learn. But for now, I'm content to watch the day gently fade with gratitude in my heart. I'm thankful for this gift of stillness. Tomorrow, I'll continue on my path, but in this moment, I'm fully present, and at peace with my soul.

BIRGITTA VISSER is a modern-day mystic, guiding others on a journey of self-discovery and empowerment. As a Soul Empowerment Coach and Divine Channel, she tunes into higher frequencies, delivering messages from the many Light Beings and Master Teachers. With her gift for Light Language Healing, she weaves light codes that activate transformation in those seeking alignment with their soul's purpose.

She is the author of *BE-com-ing Authentically Me*, sharing her often turbulent life's journey — one that has taken her through the shadows and into the light. Though her path has been anything but conventional, Birgitta's story serves as a beacon of hope and inspiration for others to unlock their own potential for growth and empowerment. Her honesty and vulnerability remind us that even in our most trying moments, we have the power to heal, overcome, and embrace our true selves.

She hopes that people will awaken to what life is all about and is simply here to offer her words as food for thought in unlocking their own potential to BE-com-ing authentically themselves.

**Tip: Switch off all distractions and simply be with yourself. Meditate, breathe, recentre, and refocus (listen to 432Hz/963Hz and/or David Ji guided meditations on YouTube)

Connect with Birgitta Visser
https://www.powersoulhealing.com
https://www.instagram.com/universallightwarriors

Alison and I connected through my podcast BECOME. We had a Zoom call where she asked me to share her experiences on my podcast. When I heard her story, it was so emotional and spot on, I said your story needs to be part of our book. And here we are. You might need a Hanky to read her story.

— Sabine Kvenberg

THROUGH TEARS & TRIUMPH: A JOURNEY OF HEALING AND EMPOWERMENT

by Allison Bladh

Challenges can indeed morph into opportunities, and in the face of hardship, there lies the potential for immense growth and evolution.

THE BITTER CHILL of a winter's night seeped through the windows, casting an icy shroud over the world outside. It was New Year's Eve, and the clock was inching towards 11 p.m. The air was heavy with anticipation, the promise of new beginnings lingering in the atmosphere. Inside the kitchen of my mother's house, the warmth from the crackling fire offered a comforting embrace against the cold outside. The room was illuminated by a soft, gentle glow, the only light source coming from a solitary lamp on the kitchen table.

After a long drive from London, I sought refuge in my mother's house. Her loyal black Labrador, ever a bundle of energy and comfort, greeted me enthusiastically, its tail wagging wildly. I settled into the chair, hoping to catch that familiar sight of my mother emerging from the kitchen with her warm smile. Yet, she wasn't there.

My mother, the heart of this cozy haven, lay in a hospital bed nearby, battling an illness that had cast its shadow over our lives. My brother had spent the entire day at her side, promising her I was on my way. She had been eager to share her plans for the coming year, plans that now seemed like echoes of a future that would never unfold.

And then my phone rang, and as my brother's voice quivered, the truth crashed over me like a relentless wave. My mother, the embodiment of love, strength, and laughter, had slipped away. The weight of her absence tightened around my heart, squeezing out the air from my lungs. She was gone before I could hold her hand and tell her how much I loved her.

From my earliest memories, my mother and I had a bond beyond words. We shared a connection that transcended the usual relationship between a parent and a child. It wasn't just mother-daughter; we were confidantes, partners in mischief, and each other's most trusted allies. The depth of our love was such that, often, words were unnecessary — a glance, a touch, a smile was all it took to communicate volumes. This bond was forged and solidified in the face of adversity. With my father's absence, a void created by his infidelity, she became the unwavering pillar of strength, wearing the dual hats of both mother and father. This shared pain, though unspoken, drew us even closer. We became a team, facing the world's challenges hand in hand. Her resilience in these moments taught me the real meaning of strength and the profound depth of a mother's love.

Reflecting on my journey, two pivotal experiences are cornerstones shaping my identity. The first was witnessing my mother's relentless navigation through the labyrinth of menopause. The second, heart-wrenching yet illuminating, was her eight-year battle against a severe illness that ultimately took her from me. Both chapters of her life showcased the incredible strength of women and taught me lessons I'll never forget. In the wake of her passing, the weight of grief compelled me to rise anew. I reinvented myself not merely as a form of healing but to serve as a bedrock of strength for other women. This transformation taught me how to channel my sorrow into purpose and resilience.

I fondly recall many moments with my mother that, upon reflection, were subtly planting the seeds of my eventual transition. One instance that stands out was when I found her standing in front of the open fridge, allowing the cool air to envelop her, a makeshift remedy for one of her intense hot flashes. Another time, she frantically searched for her glasses, a mix of confusion and amusement in her eyes, saying, "I can't for the life of me find my spectacles," only to realize—with a burst of laughter from both of us—that they were perched on her head all along. These moments, filled with humor and warmth, brought us closer and highlighted the intricate journey of womanhood that I would later delve into deeply.

Beyond these fleeting comedic interludes, a deeper narrative unfolded: her tumultuous journey through menopause. Symptoms like night sweats, inexplicable mood shifts, and fatigue tried to overshadow her luminous spirit. Though society often minimized these experiences, they painted a tale of endurance and transformation to her and me.

She'd describe her feelings many a night, enveloped in the comforting aroma of herbal teas, likening them to a rollercoaster. Observing her navigate these challenges, a fire ignited within me. I researched, suggesting dietary adjustments, meditation, and natural remedies. Each victory, however small, was our shared joy. But it wasn't just her menopausal journey that shaped me. As we navigated her subsequent illness, our bond deepened further. She wasn't just my mother; she became my pillar, confidante, and an ever-resilient inspiration. Through the highs and lows, tears and laughter, an indomitable passion for women's health was kindled within me. These raw, poignant moments lit the beacon for my future endeavors.

The day of her diagnosis remains etched in my heart. We sat together in the warmth of her sunlit living room, the golden rays casting a soft glow upon her face. A comforting aroma of freshly baked bread wafted through, yet there was a profound heaviness, a depth of emotion that was difficult to navigate. It was in this setting that she gently unfolded the news of her chronic leukemia diagnosis. The chirping of the birds outside seemed distant, their cheerful notes contrasting the heavy silence that enveloped us.

Even in this heart-wrenching moment, her inherent strength, her unyielding spirit, shone through.

As time progressed, the curtains were drawn back to reveal the disheartening reality of my mother's deteriorating health. Beyond the quiet adversities of menopause that she bravely confronted, there was now the added burden of her debilitating illness. Each day brought its own challenges, yet she faced them with an indomitable spirit that was both awe-inspiring and heart-wrenching. Witnessing her resilience in the face of such adversity instilled in me a deep sense of empathy. It wasn't just for her but for the myriad of women out there, silently traversing the intricate maze of midlife. Each has its own story and battles but deserves understanding and support. This realization fanned a flame within me, igniting a desire to make a difference and provide a guiding hand for those seeking solace in this complex phase of life.

Amidst this shadowy period, hope emerged in exploring the restorative power of nutrition and self-care. Her battle with chronic leukemia was both a physical and emotional struggle. Witnessing her vulnerability was heart-wrenching, but it paved the way to a pivotal discovery: the transformative power of nutrition. We immersed ourselves in holistic health, understanding the healing essence of food and its impact on well-being. Embracing a nutrient-rich diet and self-care practices like yoga, we observed gradual yet positive shifts in her health.

While it wasn't a miracle cure, this approach revitalized her spirit and reinforced the treatment's effectiveness. This profound experience with nutrition's healing potential spurred my journey into nutritional therapy. Amidst the anguish, my mother's ordeal inadvertently steered me toward my life's mission, underscoring that even in darkness, growth and purpose can emerge.

After witnessing the transformative power of nutrition first-hand, a newfound zeal took root within me. This was not just about managing illness but optimizing the vitality and well-being of women everywhere. I realized that if tailored nutritional advice and focused lifestyle changes could positively impact my mother's health, countless women worldwide could benefit from this holistic approach. This realization ignited a fire, compelling me to pivot my career. My prior experiences as an aesthetician, helping women with skin health, provided a unique foundation. But I knew I wanted, and needed, to do more. I decided to transition from skincare to delving deep into nutritional therapy. I became resolute in my mission: to empower and support women globally, guiding them through their unique health journeys with the healing power of nutrition.

Her absence is a constant heartache, but it has become the fire that fuels my drive. Drawing inspiration from her enduring strength and determination, I transformed my sorrow into a relentless pursuit of purpose. Instead of being ensnared by grief, I let it become the wind beneath my wings, guiding me toward a mission of making a real difference in the lives of countless women.

After intense years at university, immersing myself in the intricate world of nutrition and its deep connection to health, my career as a nutritional therapist began. The challenges and victories I witnessed alongside my mother profoundly inspired this journey. I often reflect upon two women I worked with early in my career. They stand out, not just because of the complexity of their cases, but because their battles were hauntingly familiar, echoing my mother's hardships. In their stories, I saw reflections of my mother's strength and vulnerability, reminding me why I chose this path.

First, there was a woman in her mid-thirties whose life had been turned upside down by debilitating fatigue and struggles with her weight. She came to me, teary-eyed and desperate, having visited numerous professionals before with no significant improvement. Each session was a raw testament to her resilience and desperation. The exhaustion she felt was eerily reminiscent of the nights I'd seen my mother battle her own health demons. With a custom nutrition plan and the integration of holistic practices, I watched as she transformed over a few months. The bags under her eyes lessened, and her natural energy gradually replaced the fatigue; she expressed profound gratitude, for not only had I given her the support she needed, but I had reignited her inner spark, guiding her back to a place of vitality and joy.

Next was a young mother, so consumed by IBS that even simple tasks like playing with her toddler seemed insurmountable. She described days when the pain was so intense that she felt trapped in her own body. The distress in her voice echoed the struggles my mother endured. Our sessions were filled with tears, hope, and triumph. Introducing targeted dietary adjustments and mindfulness exercises, her daily agonies began to wane. As the weeks unfolded, it was heartwarming to hear her recount stories of playing with her child or enjoying a meal without the looming dread of discomfort.

Navigating the path from my educational years to a practicing nutritional therapist was challenging. At times, the weight of responsibility and the depth of human suffering I encountered threatened to overwhelm me. Yet, in those darkest moments, the memory of my mother—her determination, her belief in healing, and the very essence of her nurturing spirit—propelled me forward. With every life touched and transformed, I wasn't just honoring my professional commitment; I was breathing life into my mother's legacy, a poignant reminder of her enduring spirit in every step forward.

While I miss my mother dearly, I am consoled by the fact that her legacy lives on, not just in my memories but in the lives of the women I help. I am a testament to her strength, courage, and unwavering belief in my potential.

This journey, from grappling with the profound loss of my mother to finding my purpose, stands as a testament to the transformative power of adversity. Challenges can indeed morph into opportunities, and in the face of hardship, there lies the potential for immense growth and evolution. As I stand here today, helping women navigate the most challenging phase of their lives, I remember my mother's words – "In every storm, find your sunshine and let it guide you, my darling." She may not be with me physically, but her spirit, resilience, and strength are my constant companions.

With each passing day, as I reach out to more women and use my knowledge and skills to make a difference, I know my journey has only begun. My story, my journey of 'Becoming,' is a testament to the power of resilience, self-belief, and the transformative power of nutrition. It's a journey I hope inspires others to embrace their challenges, to persevere, and above all, to believe in their potential. Because, in the end, that's what this life journey is all about — Becoming the best version of ourselves.

**ALISON BLADH**, an award-winning registered nutritional therapist and esthetician for over 30 years, has been helping women enhance their health and wellness, focusing on perimenopause, menopause, and beyond. Her approach blends personalized dietary, health, mindset, and lifestyle strategies to support women navigating the challenges of midlife/menopause. As a respected health writer, engaging podcast guest, sought-after speaker, and insightful webinar presenter, Alison shares her extensive expertise far and wide. She also imparts her knowledge through working as a teacher. Alison created the Menopause 5-Step Breakthrough Pathway, an innovative program to help midlife women regain their vitality. Her commitment extends beyond her professional sphere, as she finds joy in family life, culinary pursuits, and outdoor activities such as scuba diving, golfing, hiking, and beekeeping. Alison's career is a testament to her dedication to empowering women to thrive with confidence and elegance during menopause.

Connect with Alison Bladh
https://www.alisonbladh.com
https://www.instagram.com/alisonbladh

I connected with Rosalyn in a mastermind group we both were part of. When she heard about my book project, she wanted to be part of it. After she shared her story with me, I couldn't say anything less than yes. How do you deal with the loss of a child? Rosalyn's journey is a powerful testament to how we can become at peace with ourselves and the world around us.

— *Sabine Kvenberg*

QUANTUM BELONGING: EMBRACING LIFE BEYOND LIMITATIONS

by Rosalyn Rourke

Quantum Belonging is like a blank canvas, neither perfect nor imperfect, worthy or unworthy. It simple "is what is." This new okayness allows us to be with 'what is,' even if what is is the death of a beloved.

WAITING FOR THE phone to ring, my husband Phil and I sat with clenched hands. When the phone finally rang, its usual ring, a ling-a-ling, sounded foreign somehow. My hands were frozen into Phil's. Could I even answer?

"I'm sorry, ma'am," the policeman said, his voice matter of fact. "Rigor mortis has set in. We cannot revive your daughter. She's been dead too long."

Gasping for breath, I said out loud, "Did he just say what I thought he said?"

We had feared the news would not be good because we could not reach Melissa. But we did not expect her life to be over. It took weeks, maybe months before I believed our 39-year-old daughter was dead.

The word "dead" was not in my vocabulary. People with my similar A Course in Miracles and Non-Dual Direct Path background tended to use the word "transition" to imply a connection with the hereafter. I felt punched in the belly by the cop's word "dead." Somehow, I would need to make friends with that word.

Melissa had not been feeling well. She'd been tired and a bit nauseous for the past few weeks. During her last weekend, we were in frequent conversation because she continued to feel ill. Over the years, Melissa felt judged by doctors because of her body size. They often did not believe her if her blood sugar was high, and she said she had not added any sugar to her diet. So when Melissa's sister, Ally, suggested she get her blood sugar tested, Melissa was adamant that she did not need a doctor's help. We never guessed that her situation was dire.

On her last day on earth, Melissa sent a text: "Mom, I hit the lottery when I got you for a mother." Any mother would be happy to hear these words. They had special meaning for me because Melissa and I had been through a bumpy mother-daughter journey. We repeated three-plus generations of mothers judging our daughters' weight as wrong. I, too, lived through this painful nightmare with my mother and can testify that I felt unlovable and turned against myself when my mother judged my weight. I spent much of my life believing I needed to look better, be more, have more, and be smarter. The belief I was unworthy shaped my identity and influenced Melissa's identity as well. Together and separately, Melissa and I journeyed with psychotherapists, coaches, and spiritual and ancestral masters and finally ended the nightmare generational cycle around mothers and weight in our family, luckily before her unexpected death. How could she be dead when we'd reached this unimaginable sweet intimacy?

A Startling Intervention From The Beyond

In the months following Melissa's death, I was sure my life was over! The searing pain of this loss ripped through me, and life seemed painful and worthless without her. I did not attempt to soothe or dampen my agony because I thought my blistering hurt represented my love for Melissa, and I wished to pay her that tribute. With these beliefs, it felt right to hurt and condemn life with my thoughts and feelings. I considered walking into the ocean so I could reach the horizon and Melissa.

And yet, that is not what happened. Many months after Melissa passed, I was sitting on a familiar log at the beach where I could listen to the noisy surf. I felt closer to Melissa when I could see the endless horizon and hear the never-ending noise. I was wearing a sweatshirt I'd bought with Melissa on an extraordinary last trip Phil and I took with Melissa to visit the Wizarding World of Harry Potter at Universal Studios. Melissa loved Harry Potter and was thrilled to introduce us to Harry's favorite drink: Butterbeer. Together we rode the train to Hogwarts School of Witchcraft. But the happy memory of our trip turned into a knife tearing open the scar tissue around my heart. Never again could we share any of Melissa's passions.

Alone on the beach, thoughts and feelings raced together, leaving me weak and confused.

Suddenly, I experienced being shaken to and fro from the outside. It was not like feeling shaky or nervous inside. It was as if I was being forcibly shaken awake from a dream. I assure you I was not hallucinating. The shaking seemed to last a few seconds and left me startled but very awake. The daggers in my heart that had been with me in various degrees for months suddenly were gone. I knew I was grounded in reality because I could remember that Melissa was dead, but her death had stopped hurting! I hadn't done anything to get this relief: no spiritual practices or mindset techniques. This new peace came unbidden, but the shaking woke me and became my kinesthetic wisdom teacher. I knew for the first time how to experience suffering one moment and the next second feel set free. I did wonder where the suffering had gone. But it was indeed gone.

My next thoughts were, "How can I be this 'okay'? Mothers who love and lose their daughters must suffer, right? Isn't grief the price we pay for love?" Society teaches us there is only one way to show love for the one who has transitioned. I had loved Melissa, I still loved Melissa, so how could I be okay? Could I admit this "okayness" to anyone or would I be excluded from the tribe of mothers who'd lost daughters?

Being okay implied that I was enough, even though Melissa was gone. The thoughts and feelings of needing to be more, look better, have more, and be smarter that had always been with me had disappeared. These feelings of lack belonged to an identity of a person who saw themselves as separate from others and the larger universe.

After the shaking, I no longer felt myself as separate from anyone or anything. Instead of experiencing myself as limited to my body-mind, I felt the aliveness of Presence that was more than me and extended to a connection beyond myself. I'd experienced a Quantum Belonging, or as some may say, Oneness, a peaceful space where the mind is at rest.

We all have moments when we drift into the sensation of being alive with okayness without concern for our looping thoughts of problems or perceived lack. For example, when a severe headache or fever leaves us, we might become aware of the presence of joy, about simply feeling okay. That okayness after the headache is gone is usually a kind of gratitude toward what has happened and the consequent relief. This is an experience of Quantum Belonging. In the space of Quantum Belonging, we are connected to "what is," and the mind has stopped repeatedly creating distorted beliefs about why and where we do not belong. When we let go of the psychological suffering these distorted, looping beliefs bring, Quantum Belonging is found in the empty, space-like place that remains. Our essence shines with this connection to belonging, and our minds are free of a running list of our attributes or flaws. Quantum Belonging is like a blank canvas, neither perfect nor imperfect, worthy or unworthy. It simply "is what is." This new okayness allows us to be with 'what is,' even if what is is the death of a beloved.

At first, I named this new calm "home." I now understand what felt like "my" home is a Quantum Belonging available to everyone at any time. I did not know it was possible to let go of looping thoughts and feelings and relax into what initially seemed like nothingness. Upon visiting this empty space more often, the silence that exists when the noise of psychological suffering is removed becomes very satisfying, like a causeless embrace from beyond. This causeless joy feels like the okayness of our true nature.

The energetic space of Quantum Belonging is similar to the natural, peaceful state we experience in the moments before we slip off into sleep: we are not fully awake, but we let go of our day's happenings and welcome rest. From this space, we're energized and filled when we re-enter the activity of the outer world. When I get over-involved with a feeling or thought in life, I return home to Quantum Belonging.

Redefining Home and Embodied Love

It has now been five and a half years since the shaking. I could not explain those moments on the beach, but afterward, I could not go back to suffering or pretend to be in the stages of grief the rest of the world seemed to expect. The shaking had taught me that my old condemning, looping thoughts and feelings had produced my psychological suffering and that the freedom of Quantum Belonging was available to me in the absence of the old mind pattern. The external facts were still the same: Melissa was dead, but it no longer hurt to think of her because I did not believe I needed to suffer to show my love for Melissa or to feel consonant on the outside and inside.

After the shaking, if I had a hurtful thought, whether it be about grief, unworthiness, comparison, or weight, instead of engaging with it, I noticed it, named it as perceived guilt or imagined unworthiness, but I no longer believed that these passing energies were who or what I am. Who I am is what is underneath these patterns. By not interacting with the mind's creations and standing as witness to them, the doorway to Quantum Belonging is always available.

I came upon Quantum Belonging through suffering, but it is available to all of us right now without suffering. If we were taught that thoughts and feelings are transitory, not the truth of our essence, we would know that we could move from fleeting thoughts or feelings to the peace of Quantum Belonging in milliseconds. Every child could be taught to withdraw interest in false ideas like imagined unworthiness. Imagined unworthiness causes us to feel as though we do not belong. When we believe in unworthiness, a disconnection with others and life seems to follow naturally, and this keeps us from knowing and believing our place is in Quantum Belonging. These feelings block us from knowing our true nature. If we learned to disengage from hurtful, conditioned thinking as children, we could know we are always at home. When we open to the knowing that our experience of okayness in Quantum Belonging is our true nature, our expression in the outer world becomes more powerful and creative because false beliefs do not armor us.

A New Perspective: Quantum Belonging in Action

I want to share an example of letting go of hurtful looping thoughts and feelings. I recently attended an event where it is traditional to recognize authors and their recently published books. A stage was set up at the front of the room with a 6X8-foot TV screen. One by one each author's headshot and book cover was projected as they were called onto the stage to discuss their book. I was sure my name would be called because my book: When Wisdom Arrives: From Imagined Unworthiness to Freedom became a bestseller last month. My name was not called. A sting shot through my heart and poisoned my thoughts for a few seconds. "Maybe the leader and the publisher thought my book was not as good as the others?" I told myself.

Once I noticed this was an old type of thought, I was in a position not to join the original thought with more of the same. Instead, I named the feeling, in this case, imagined unworthiness, and asked myself, "Am I okay if the book is not presented on stage?" An emphatic "yes" arose inside me, and I felt a new impulse to stand taller with my shoulders back because of this okayness, knowing my essence wouldn't change whether my book was showcased or not.

Moments later, when the event leader crossed my path, I simply asked, "Do you plan to have my book on stage?"

"My intuition was to have you on stage tomorrow," she replied.

Before experiencing Quantum Belonging, I would have felt too unworthy and embarrassed to ask for my book to be shared because I expected rejection and "knew" I did not belong. But Quantum Belonging showed me that becoming aware of hurtful thoughts and feelings and not believing them is a powerful experience of freedom. The portal to "home" comes through the thought interruption of the belief that we are "not yet" worthy. When we release the seesaw of our hurtful thoughts and beliefs, there is an opening for all to enter the sweet energy of Quantum Belonging.

An Invitation For You To Find A Home in Quantum Belonging

Today, I treasure my daughter and live expansively in her memory within the context that we both (and all!) have memberships in Quantum Belonging. I continue to claim Quantum Belonging as home. Best Selling Author, Speaker, Master Enneagram Teacher, and Oneness Coach are the perks of not listening to my old, con-demning thoughts and my belief that "mothers who love their daughters need to suffer." Everyone belongs to an ultimate, calm, unwavering, infinite reality. I am here to invite you to join me in the ultimate destination: knowing our Quantum Belonging. From here, everything is possible because our lives are restored by knowing that, at our essence, we all are part of a Connected Existence. Belonging results from stepping out of old beliefs of imagined unworthiness and into everyone's birthright: ultimate belonging. Are you ready to shift and take a stand for your new home? I look forward to continuing this conversation with you at rosalynrourke.com

Best-selling author **ROSALYN ROURKE**, MSW, has worked deeply in the field of mental health and trauma therapy as a psychotherapist. With a Master's degree from Smith College School for Social Work in 1973, she embarked on a distinguished career that included supervisory roles in Yale Psychiatric Facilities. Her expertise further expanded as she immersed herself in trauma work, particularly Eye Movement Desensitization Reprogramming (EMDR), a highly effective PTSD treatment. In 1995, she pursued advanced training in eating disorders, focusing on binge eating and body dysmorphia.

An avid learner, Rosalyn's professional and personal journey into transformation led her to the Enneagram, where she studied under renowned mentors such as Tom Condon, Don Riso, and Russ Hudson, among others. Her influential work extends to the literary realm with her best-selling book, *When Wisdom Arrives: From Imagined Unworthiness to Freedom*. Rosalyn continues to inspire and empower individuals on their path to self-discovery and freedom as an Oneness Coach.

On her website, you will find dedicated meditations and a Q&A to help you experience Quantum Belonging! Follow her on Facebook, Instagram, TikTok and YouTube.

To join Rosalyn in breaking free from intergenerational trauma, unworthiness beliefs, and loneliness issues of not belonging, please contact her below.

Connect with Rosalyn Rourke
https://www.rosalynrourke.com
https://www.instagram.com/rosalynrourke

I was in the middle of finalizing the chapters of my book when I got an unexpected phone call from Rena. A friend told her about the Become Book project and said to call Sabine. I knew Rena. We met twice briefly, but I never knew her story. Once she shared it, I was hooked. This must be told, I replied. She became the lucky number 13 co-author. Her story was featured on CNN, Good Morning America, Nightline, The Doctors Show, PBS, FOX-TV, NBC-TV, Woman's World Magazine, and The Epoch Times.

— *Sabine Kvenberg*

A SHATTERED FANTASY WORLD: FINDING MY INNER LIGHT

by Rena Greenberg

When you follow your passion and stay connected to your highest Source of Truth within, you can truly overcome any obstacle and create a life that is so much bigger than you.

SINCE THE AGE of 17, my life in New York City has been like a dream. Fast-paced. Fun. Full of excitement. It included celebrity, travel, and friendship. A welcome reprieve from a childhood ripe with trauma. Suddenly, at 26 years of age, my NYC fantasy world was shattered.

Born in Forest Hills, NY, my parents were both immigrants. My father's family had escaped Ukraine and Russia (at the time) with only the shirts on their backs. They were fleeing in terror from religious persecution. My Grandmother had watched as her father was pulled by his legs onto the front lawn of their home and shot and killed right before her very eyes during the pogroms of the early 1900s.

My father's family took refuge in Palestine. They had left all their belongings and wealth in Russia, and they were now dirt poor. When I met my grandparents in Israel at the age of 7, I was struck by the poverty in which his family lived. They didn't even have a bathroom, just an outhouse.

I was proud of my father's tenacity. At a young age, he learned English and then started teaching English as a way to make money. He was accepted into the Technion, one of the best Engineering schools in the world. After excelling in this well-respected Israeli school, my father received a full scholarship to Columbia University. That was his ticket out of the slums of Jerusalem to New York City and a second chance—an opportunity to build a new life in America.

There was only one problem. His past trauma had left him deeply emotionally and mentally scarred at a time in history when these types of issues were mostly ignored. He didn't know he needed help in this area and did not seek any.

He met my Mother in NYC. My Mother is a German Jew. At the age of 12, her Mother, my Grandmother Ilse, had the courage to put my Mother and her brother on the Kindertransport. The Kindertransport was a program made possible by the generosity of the Quakers. As Hitler made clear his plan to eradicate all Jews, the Quakers intervened by going to the German government and begging them to "at least let the children go." They agreed, and the Kindertransport was born.

A lovely British family adopted my Mother during the war. When my Grandmother was finally able to flee Germany, she could not go to England to be with her children as she had hoped.

Fortunately, my Grandmother was able to come to the United States. She arrived with only $11 in her pocket and took a room in a crowded NYC apartment. Ilse (my Grandmother) immediately began working in a factory to make ends meet.

When my mother was 18, she was finally reunited with her mother. My mother crossed the Atlantic Ocean by boat from England and arrived in a new city and a new country, all of which were very foreign to her. Once in the USA, my mother threw herself into her education, where she flourished, attending Hunter College in NYC and then getting a scholarship to Smith College and the Sorbonne in Paris.

My mother met my father while standing in line at a cafeteria in Manhattan. His can-do nature appealed to her, coupled with the fact that he was also foreign and Jewish. After a one-year courtship, they married. They had three children, and I was in the middle.

My childhood was fraught with anxiety. I never knew when my father would have an outburst. My mother was terrified of his rage. So was I. When my father's attacks became violent, my sisters and I would hold up a big chair as a barrier to prevent him from beating my mother.

When his ire was directed 100% towards me, I would hide in my room, lock the door and cover the protruding knob with masking tape to prevent him from breaking in. Still, he would find a way to break that lock in the middle of the night and come barreling towards me in a rage while I cowered in my bed.

My silver lining was my inborn faith. I do not know what I thought of it, as I had rejected all my religious "education," but I felt I was in consistent communication with the Divine. I wrote to my Higher Power, whom I called God, and felt a frequent response. I prayed for strength, friends, and new opportunities. I cultivated my inner light and was blessed with beautiful friendships. Unlike my mother, I rejected academics. I never expected to go to college.

One day, sitting around in Art class at Franklin High School in Somerset, New Jersey, I found myself browsing through a box full of college catalogs. I stumbled upon a catalog for the Fashion Institute of Technology (FIT). I felt a surge of excitement. The school was in New York City. The teachers were professionals from the fashion, advertising, and design industry. I immediately felt an inner knowing that going to this unique school in the city known as The Big Apple was my destiny.

I went to tell my guidance counselor the good news, who abruptly told me, "No one from Franklin High School ever got into the Fashion Institute of Technology (F.I.T)." I knew that I would be the exception. I didn't know how.

I began to put together my portfolio. I had won two art contests while in high school. The prize for one of them was that I got to paint a mural on an elementary school library wall. Every day after my classes, I walked over to Pine Grove Elementary, where I climbed a ladder to reach the wall above tall bookshelves and painted the animated figures I had created.

Photos of that project became the keystone of my portfolio to gain acceptance into F.I.T. After submitting my portfolio and essay, I eagerly ran to the mailbox every day after school, anxious to hear my fate. One day a letter arrived letting me know that my dream had come true: I got into F.I.T. and was moving to NYC. I cried tears of gratitude and ecstatic joy. My dream came true.

My life in NYC was more amazing than I could have dreamed possible. After graduating from FIT, I got really fun jobs—working in fashion, entertainment, and travel. I met the most interesting people and enjoyed all the diversity and excitement New York City had to offer.

Then, all of a sudden, it was as if someone pulled the plug. I lost all my energy. Gone. I was exhausted and felt like I was now existing in a black cloud of extreme fatigue. I had no idea what was wrong with me. I started pounding the pavement in New York City, going from doctor to doctor, searching for answers and frantically seeking a solution. I felt desperate.

After a year of this, no one found anything, and I assumed my "illness" must be all in my head, even though I was so exhausted I could barely lift my head off the pillow. I had to push myself just to get through the day.

Trying to continue with my life, I saw an acupuncturist. He told me that he could not treat me because my pulse was skipping beats. He advised me to go to the emergency room.

The next afternoon I walked to Brooklyn Methodist Hospital. I expected to be turned away. Instead, I was whisked into the emergency room, hooked up to monitors and machines, and was told I needed to be admitted.

"I can't be admitted," I protested, "I'm too busy." That was when I had my first wake-up call. A lovely Swedish doctor leaned in and said to me earnestly, "This is so serious. The only thing keeping you alive is your age. Your heart is beating at only 30 beats per minute."

I was admitted into the cardiac care unit, where I lay in bed for three weeks. While in the CCU, the chief of cardiology put a catheter up to my heart and peered at it with a dye. A room full of Physician Residents gazed on when the Chief Cardiologist announced that I had the heart of an 80-year-old. I was only 26 years old at the time.

The doctor attached a temporary pacemaker and put me back in CCU for observation. While there, I had a heart attack with pain radiating down my left arm and throughout my chest. The next day, the Chief of Cardiology implanted a permanent pacemaker into my chest.

When I was finally discharged from the hospital 3 weeks later, I remember standing on the streets of Park Slope, Brooklyn, feeling so grateful to be alive. "I had a second chance!"

As far as my health, I still didn't feel great, even with a permanent pacemaker bringing my heart rhythm up to where it needed to be. I still felt tired with brain fog too much of the time. I realized that if I were to get healthy, I needed to take my health into my own hands. I started studying everything I could about health.

Discovering Mind-Body Healing

After the pacemaker was implanted in my heart, and I still felt sick, I realized that the medical profession was limited in how it could help me. The first real turning point for me was discovering hypnotic biofeedback.

Through that exposure, I began to understand the two branches of the nervous system—sympathetic and parasympathetic—or fight or flight response, and how it related to me.

Though the origin of my "illness" was unknown, though likely caused by a parasite or virus I had contracted while traveling, by activating the relaxation response more of the time, I found that I felt better and was less tired.

I wanted to find a way to reduce my body's stress response by activating the "relaxation response" more often and not being dependent on external machines or devices.

It was evident that the solution would be training my mind to influence my body's responses in a way that would promote healing and allow me to transform unproductive habits into a positive lifestyle (healthy eating and moderate exercise, healthy relationships, coupled with relaxation).

The problem I found with biofeedback alone was that it was limited because it didn't have a mechanism to reprogram your mind to create a positive change in habits.

Coming up with Easy Willpower

That's when I came up with the methods I later coined, the "Easy Willpower" and "Dynamic Mind" self-hypnosis strategy. I feel like it was this system that moved the needle for me, finally!

My method combined Neuro-Linguistic Programming (NLP) with biofeedback, energy healing, body awareness training, and hypnosis to reprogram my mind to quit sugar and alcohol (and end all my addictions) and be in a relaxed "meditative healing" state, where I could access my "wise-mind" more often.

I hadn't thought this was possible as my lifestyle had revolved around consuming sugar (in its many forms) and trying to cope with anxiety unconsciously.

But the re-programming self-hypnosis gave me the confidence to see myself, my life, the substances I had been "addicted" to, and food in a new way that strengthened me.

I was consciously increasing my awareness to breathe more fully, catch my limited thinking, and reverse it, while actively using imagery and awareness of energy to create a brighter future and release the trauma that had lodged in the cells of my body.

My new vitality probably came from my new eating habits and lifestyle, but I couldn't have achieved either without the self-hypnosis methods I had developed. The inner work gave me the strength, "willpower," and resilience to make the changes in my outer world.

That's why the wellness program I then developed for hospitals and corporations that I brought to millions of people online and over 200,000 people face-to-face in seminars throughout the country featured dynamic-mind self-hypnosis rather than nutrition.

As important as nutritional education is, I realized that all the knowledge in the world couldn't have made a difference for me until I was finally motivated, not just consciously but subconsciously, to make the changes I needed to make.

Dynamic Mind and Easy Willpower—the methods I developed gave me both the motivation and the tools for transformation.

I now had the willpower and skill to change my thoughts, emotional patterns, and my lifestyle. The amazing side benefit was that I got healthy.

I learned that the deep inner heart, the seat of the subconscious mind, is the only place where true change can happen. We must go beyond the repetitive voices in our heads and limited pictures in our minds to access the deepest resources for healing within.

Though herbs and superfoods also played a big role in my healing, specifically the herbs/superfoods I later used in the herbal elixirs I created for Rena's Organic.

The blessings that came into my life through my healing process were beyond anything I could have ever imagined.

While I was still in New York, recovering from the unknown illness that had caused my heart to almost stop beating, I started studying everything I could about health to try to find a way to heal myself.

Little did I know that the knowledge I would acquire would propel me to start my own wellness program to help thousands. A few years later, I moved to Sarasota, Florida, where I founded Wellness Seminars, Inc. Over 75 hospitals and 100+ corporations brought me on-site to help their employees lose weight and stop smoking.

Hundreds of my successful clients came forward, wanting to share their amazing weight loss and smoking cessation results. The local and national media were thirsty to share these success stories.

Soon I was getting calls from people worldwide who were seeking help in all areas of their lives and wanted to use my method to assist them. CNN, Good Morning America, Nightline, The Doctors Show, PBS, FOX-TV, NBC-TV, Woman's World Magazine, and The Epoch Times all featured me and my clients' success in their news stories.

This outcome was beyond my wildest dreams. I learned that when you follow your passion and stay connected to your highest Source of Truth within, you can truly overcome any obstacle and create a life that is so much bigger than you.

My greatest life lesson has been the consistent reinforcement of this fact I've come to know—you and I are not alone. One of my

Spiritual teachers spoke Truth so beautifully when she said: "God is the Ocean. The people (and events) are the rivers." Rivers do dry up, but the Source never does. Staying connected to Source, within my own Heart and Soul, is the essence of what I have learned and am here to teach.

Rena Greenberg's success with weight loss and addiction has been featured in 160+ TV and news stories, including USA Today, Woman's World Magazine, The Doctor's Show, CNN, FOX-TV, Good Morning America, and ABC-TV Nightline, including her own show on PBS.

RENA GREENBERG. Since 1990, Rena's wellness program has been reviewed and sponsored in over 75 United States hospitals and 100+ major corporations, including Disney, Home Depot and AT&T. Rena is the creator of Rena's Organic, a premier, medical-grade line of nutritional products.

Hay House Author, Rena Greenberg holds a degree in bio-psychology from the City University of New York and a master's degree from the University of Spiritual Healing and Sufism. She is also a hypnotherapy and NLP trainer and is board-certified in biofeedback therapy.

Rena has helped over 200,000 people change their lives, with her hospital-based wellness program and now her medical-grade herbal product line, Rena's Organic.

Connect with Rena Greenberg
www.EasyWillpower.com
www.RenasOrganic.com

EPILOGUE

LIKE MANY OF you, after reading these remarkable stories of triumph and strength, I understand that we all go through experiences in life that define us. No matter if it is to find our purpose, extend forgiveness, or find the love for ourselves and others.

Like the humble caterpillar, we often mirror the transformative path of a caterpillar evolving into a butterfly. We begin our life's journey with a narrow view, limited to the world we see immediately around us. The caterpillar's transformation within its cocoon resembles those pivotal, introspective times when we face challenges and personal growth. These moments might feel solitary and intense, as if we are enveloped in our cocoons, grappling with inner changes unseen by the world. Yet, this metamorphosis is crucial. As the caterpillar emerges as a magnificent butterfly, so too do we emerge from these experiences, having gained wisdom, resilience, and a new perspective. Much like the butterfly, our transformation is a profound evolution of our soul. It enables us to embrace life's varied experiences with newfound grace and strength. The butterfly's journey reminds us that each stage of life, with its hardships and triumphs, contributes to the beautiful and unique tapestry of our existence.

When I look for the silver lining, I realize that it is how we communicate not only with others but also with ourselves that matters. What we say, how we say it, and how we respond to the challenges life gives us will affect the results we experience, and what our lives become will impact others.

That evening, when I overcame the fear of performing my original song, a woman approached me, saying she needed to hear my message. Her words gave me the courage to continue my speaking career. I realized then that if I could touch one person, that person could impact many others, starting a ripple effect. When we become great communicators, we can change the world one person at a time.

Once we reach self-actualization by following our dreams and living on purpose — there is no turning back to the old way of thinking and doing.

We all begin like "Caterpillas". We start crawling, but when we understand that a transformation has to happen to get to the next level in life and let it happen, we will take to the sky and flap our beautiful wings.

Once we become the person we are meant to be, we can live the life we are destined to live.